beadmaille

beadmaille

Jewelry with Bead Weaving & Metal Rings

Cindy Thomas Pankopf

LARK BOOKS

A Division of Sterling Publishing Co., Inc.
New York / London

Senior Editor: TERRY TAYLOR

Editor: LARRY SHEA

Art Director: KATHLEEN HOLMES

Junior Designer: CAROL MORSE

Illustrator: CINDY THOMAS PANKOPF

Photographer: STEWART O'SHIELDS

Cover Designer: CELIA NARANJO

Library of Congress Cataloging-in-Publication Data

Pankopf, Cindy Thomas.
  Beadmaille : jewelry with bead weaving & metal rings / Cindy Thomas Pankopf. -- 1st ed.
    p. cm.
  Includes index.
  ISBN 978-1-60059-495-3 (pb-trade pbk. : alk. paper)
  1. Jewelry making. 2. Beadwork. 3. Weaving. I. Title.
  TT212.P35 2010
  739.27--dc22

                                    2009039385
10 9 8 7 6 5 4 3 2 1

First Edition

Published by Lark Books, A Division of Sterling Publishing Co., Inc.
387 Park Avenue South, New York, NY 10016

Distributed in Canada by Sterling Publishing,
c/o Canadian Manda Group, 165 Dufferin Street
Toronto, Ontario, Canada M6K 3H6

Distributed in the United Kingdom by GMC Distribution Services,
Castle Place, 166 High Street, Lewes, East Sussex, England BN7 1XU

Distributed in Australia by Capricorn Link (Australia) Pty Ltd.,
P.O. Box 704, Windsor, NSW 2756 Australia

If you have questions or comments about this book, please contact:
Lark Books
67 Broadway
Asheville, NC 28801
828-253-0467

Manufactured in China

ISBN 13: 978-1-60059-495-3

For information about custom editions, special sales, and premium and corporate purchases, please contact the Sterling Special Sales Department at 800-805-5489 or specialsales@sterlingpub.com.

For information about desk and examination copies available to college and university professors, requests must be submitted to academic@larkbooks.com. Our complete policy can be found at www.larkbooks.com.

contents

INTRODUCTION	6
THE BASICS	8
MATERIALS	8
TOOLS	12
TECHNIQUES	15

THE PROJECTS

Art Deco Necklace	22
Beadmaille Necklace	26
Centipede Bracelet	31
Celtic Lace Necklace	34
Caterpillar Bracelet	39
Accordion Cuff	42
Clover Leaf Ensemble	46
Cherry Blossom Ensemble	52
Cleopatra Necklace	58
Copper Clusters Lariat	64
Triad Ring	69
Foxtail Necklace	73
Faerie Garden Necklace	80
Identical Triplets Necklace	84
London Flat Bracelet	88
Spiral Chain Necklace	92
Two-Tone Doublewide Cuff	96
Seashell Pendant	100
X Factor Bracelet	104
Zinnia Necklace	108
Zinnia Bracelet	112
Diamond Ring	117
Musubu Earrings	121

ACKNOWLEDGMENTS	124
ABOUT THE AUTHOR	125
INDEX	126

introduction

I'LL ADMIT IT—I'M JUST A LITTLE BIT OBSESSIVE when it comes to beading. Okay, a lot obsessive. Beading, or at least thinking about beading, is something I never take a vacation from. And thank goodness for that, or the book you're holding wouldn't exist.

The technique featured in this book got its start when I was in a hotel room on a family vacation and an idea came to me. I simply had to find a store to buy some beads and try it out. (I always seem to be dragging my family to places they don't consider part of the actual vacation.) The design I imagined used right-angle weave to make interlocking strips of woven beads. The result was so terrific that I knew right away I wanted to do more with it. Back home, I discovered some beautiful textured rings and thought about combining those rings with the interlocking strips of right-angle weave.

That was the beginning of my obsession with what I've come to call *beadmaille*—combining bead-stitching techniques and metal rings to reinterpret traditional chainmail designs. Beadmaille uses seed beads structurally, replacing some of the rings in chainmail patterns. Once I began exploring this concept, ideas kept flowing and, before I knew it, this book was born.

As I started creating beadmaille, I discovered that the jewelry designs it led me to were all linked together, just like the pieces I was making. The first one I designed was the Beadmaille Necklace (page 26), a variation on the traditional European chainmail pattern. You'll be intrigued by the way the beading traps and supports the decorative rings. Next, I experimented with a base of beadwork using open jump rings in patterns that go around and through the beading, and the Copper Clusters Lariat (page 64) and X Factor Bracelet (page 104) appeared. When I explored Celtic chainmail, I realized it adapts easily to bead and jump ring layers; the Cherry Blossom Ensemble (page 52) is a beautiful example. All the projects here—from necklaces and bracelets to rings and pendants—incorporate variations of European or Japanese patterns in their construction.

These projects are designed for both bead weaving and chainmail enthusiasts looking to try something new. Beadmaille truly is a unique hybrid of the two techniques. Metal rings add a whole new feel to seed bead jewelry, as the additional weight makes each piece much more substantial and luxurious. And if you're a chainmail artist, you can now add limitless colors and a touch of softness to your jewelry.

Whatever your past experience, don't be afraid to jump right in and start creating! If you've never done any chainmail before, try the Caterpillar Bracelet (page 39). It features two colors of seed beads combined in a single strip of right-angle weave with contrasting jump rings. This is a quick-to-stitch project that will get you comfortable with working with jump rings. The result looks much more complicated than it really is. If you're new to beading, the Celtic Lace Necklace (page 34) is a great introduction, with no needle and thread required. Because the seed beads are strung on flexible beading wire, it's a snap to work the traditional Celtic chainmail through the beaded rings.

I hope you enjoy exploring, creating, and wearing beadmaille as much as I do. Let the skills you learn here motivate you to create your own new designs and help you to find inspiration in unexpected places. And when inspiration suddenly hits you, I hope the bead store is still open and not too far away, and that you have a family as understanding as mine. I'd like to think that anything resulting in gorgeous, unique jewelry can only be considered a healthy obsession.

the basics

Creating beadmaille is an innovative concept, a marriage of bead weaving and chainmail techniques. Don't worry if you aren't familiar with certain elements of either technique. This section will tell you everything you need to know about the materials, tools, and techniques required to successfully create these truly unique designs. I will share tips, secrets, and things to watch out for that I discovered while creating these designs and while teaching this technique to others. I suggest that you begin by making the designs as specified in the projects, then experiment to create pieces in your own particular style.

Materials

Beads, wire, thread, and more . . . read on for descriptions of all the items that are used to create each of the projects in this book.

Beads

Traditional chainmail projects are typically made entirely of metal rings. All of the projects in *Beadmaille* are constructed with a combination of metal jump rings and linking rings made of beads of all kinds. I've specified the type and size of the beads for each project that are critical to the success of each piece. Using beads other than those recommended will adversely affect the finished product.

Seed beads

Seed beads, also known as *rocailles*, are the reason I started beading in the first place. The first time I walked through the door of a bead store and saw all of those beautiful tiny things in so many magnificent colors, I was hooked. I grabbed a book and started stitching them into bracelets immediately. I went through a period when my husband, Mike, would come home from work and ask me, "How many did you make today?" (I don't think things are much different now!)

Seed beads get their name from their slightly bulging seed-like shape. They come in an array of sizes, defined by a number—the bigger the number, the smaller the bead. They range from 20° (extra tiny, several would fit on the head of a pin) to 2° (about 6 mm wide). Most of the projects in this book use size 11° beads, which are about 1.5 mm wide.

All seed beads are not created equal, as even those of the same designated size have lots of variation in size and shape. Some are squat like donuts, while others are much taller with straighter sides like a marshmallow. There are a few basic types you'll find in most bead shops:

Czech seed beads are usually sold in hanks, have a rather squat profile, and a lot more variation in size and shape from bead to bead. While they are beautiful when strung, I don't recommend them for any of these projects.

Japanese seed beads are the most uniform in size and shape, so they are the only beads I use in beadmaille. They are typically sold in tubes or bags. Matte, transparent, opaque, shiny, or metallic . . . the options are endless, but even within the realm of Japanese seed beads, there are beads to avoid because of their size. For instance, silver-lined square-holed beads are lovely, but a real problem to work with because they tend to be just a touch bigger than usual. I once made a Centipede Bracelet (page 31) with silver-lined square-holed beads because I thought it would not affect the fit of the jump rings, which was true. However, the finished bracelet was about an inch (2.5 cm) longer than it was supposed to be!

Japanese cylinder beads have large holes and straight sides, and they are slightly smaller than seed beads of the same designated size. Some common cylinder beads are Miyuki Delicas and Toho Treasures. In general, they aren't interchangeable with seed beads but are called for in certain projects where their size and shape are necessary.

Other beads

Seed beads are used as the backbone to beadmaille, but you'll need some other beads to embellish and further beautify your designs.

Japanese drop beads could technically be called seed beads, but they are used primarily in this book for embellishing. They are 3.4 mm wide, much like a size 6° seed bead with an off-kilter hole. This type of drop is smaller than the drop beads typically sold on strands in bead stores. Because of the size difference, they are not interchangeable with other drop beads.

Focal beads add visual interest to some of the pieces in this book. They are usually the largest bead in the design, drawing attention right away, and can be made out of any material, including glass or gemstone. *Lampworked focal beads* are handmade by melting glass rods in a torch flame, then wrapping the molten glass around a metal rod called a mandrel. These stunning pieces of art are the perfect focal point to many beadmaille designs. Semiprecious gemstones would also make lovely focal beads.

Accent beads are the many different types of beads used to accentuate some of the projects in this book. I've used *semiprecious gemstone beads*; *crystal beads*, made of faceted leaded glass; and *Czech glass beads*, which come in all different shapes, sizes, and finishes.

Spacer beads, usually made of metal, add a touch of sparkle and nice detail. Daisy spacers are the smallest type; they are little flat discs that look like daisies. Any small filler bead could be considered a spacer bead.

Findings

Findings are the usually metal pieces that finish off a project. There are hundreds of types, but you'll only need to know these for the projects in this book:

Crimp beads allow you to securely fasten off flexible beading wire. There are different types for different situations: *Round crimp beads* are designed to be squashed flat with a pair of chain-nose pliers. *Tubular crimp beads* can be smashed flat with chain-nose pliers or turned into cylinders with crimping pliers.

Wire protectors or *wire guards* protect flexible beading wire and thread at the end of a piece from abrading and wearing. The horseshoe shape fits neatly through the loop portion of clasps. To add a wire protector, pass the stringing material through one side, down through the other side, then through the clasp loop. Finish as if the stringing material was wrapping directly around the clasp.

Bead caps are decorative, cupped metal findings designed to cradle another bead. They come in many sizes to fit different-sized beads.

Clasps are used to connect the ends of a piece. There are numerous types of clasps available, from *sliding bar clasps* to *toggles*, *box clasps*, *S-hooks*, and *lobster claws*. I use them all.

Bails are used to hang a pendant from a necklace. *Pinch bails* have little prongs inside. To use a pinch bail, simply open it up, pinch it closed so the prongs fit into the hole of a top-drilled pendant, and hang.

Ear wires connect an earring to the ear lobe. Personal preference plays a huge role in determining what type of ear wire to select. *Fishhooks* are easy to insert; *posts* are great for heavy earrings; and *leverbacks* are very secure. All come in metals to match your project.

Jump rings are open circles of wire used to create chainmail, but they are also used for linking other findings to jewelry. Standard-size jump rings are easy to make (see Making Jump Rings, page 21), but they are also easy to find commercially. Bead shops usually carry a large selection, but you might also consider checking online chainmail sources to get just the size and type of metal you'd like. When purchasing rings, be sure to specify the diameter and gauge of wire of the ring. Most chainmail sources measure the inner diameter or *I.D.* This measurement indicates the hole size of the jump ring, which is very different from the outer diameter, or *O.D.,* of the entire ring. In this book, you'll find most jump rings are measured by the I.D. in the materials lists. It's important to stick by this measurement because the difference between, say, a 4-mm I.D. ring and a 4-mm O.D. ring can be 2 mm! Jump rings can be made with different thicknesses of wire, or gauge. In this book, jump rings and wire are measured by the American Wire Gauge system.

Decorative rings are closed, textured circles that come in different metals, finishes, sizes, shapes, and textures. In beadmaille they're incorporated into the beadweaving for structure and decorative effect. Most bead stores have rings available or can get them for you. They're also available online.

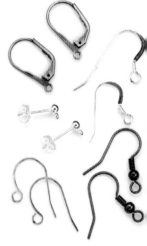

Stringing Materials

Various beadmaille designs require stringing materials with different characteristics. Key attributes to look for are strength, drape, and color.

Braided beading thread is the thread that I use most often because it has exceptional strength for its size. Although it's designed for the fishing industry, this type of thread has characteristics that are also great for beading: It's super strong, doesn't tangle easily, knots well, and the 6-pound (2.7 k) thread is only 0.15 mm wide. Happily, it's available at most bead stores, usually in two colors: smoke and crystal. Smoke is the best for most applications. Because it's a little darker, it blends into the shadows and disappears. If the beads you've selected are very light or transparent in color, use crystal so the thread doesn't affect the color of your beads. Crystal does appear white in finished pieces, which is much more apparent than the smoke.

This type of thread comes in different weights, which aren't interchangeable. I typically call for the 6-, 8-, or 10-pound (2.7, 3.6, and 4.5 k) varieties. Certain projects support much more ring weight and require a sturdier thread, while others need a lighter weight to be able to fit multiple passes of thread through the beads.

Nylon beading thread was developed for the upholstery industry. It's typically sold on bobbins and comes in a variety of colors and weights. Size D is a good thread width for these projects. Nylon beading thread is not as stiff as braided beading thread, so it's good to use when you've got less ring weight and want the piece to have more drape. Nylon beading thread is also useful when you're making numerous passes of thread though the same beads, or when the thread shows a lot. Always be sure to stretch and condition this type of thread before use. To stretch it, simply unspool about 1 yard (.9 m), wind a bit around both index fingers and pull taut. Hold for about three seconds, then move down the thread and repeat.

Thread conditioner, though not a stringing material, is used to tame your thread. I use a synthetic conditioner with smoke-colored braided beading thread to help keep the smoke color on the line instead of my fingers. I also feel that its tackiness helps keep the beads in place as I stitch. With nylon beading thread, it's absolutely necessary to condition after you stretch it. It will help prevent tangling, fraying, and a lot of frustration.

Flexible beading wire is the type of stringing material I use for my most substantial beadmaille pieces. Its nylon-coated, steel construction provides the ultimate in strength. Higher-quality beading wire has more internal steel strands (I use 49-strand wire). These wires are less likely to kink and are fluid, not stiff like wires with fewer strands. I wouldn't use anything less than a 19-strand wire. Regardless of the number

Needle Threading Tips

• Smash the end of fishing line with a pair of pliers. This will make it nice and flat so it will easily slide through the eye of the needle.

• Use a black permanent marker on the end of crystal fishing line so you can see it.

• Pinch the thread between the index finger and thumb of your non-dominant hand. Slide it down until it looks like a tiny splinter. Hold the needle in your dominant hand. Slide the eye down over the "splinter" of thread. Done!

Each flexible beading wire manufacturer uses a proprietary coating on their products, and each feels different. Because they're all different, you'll want to use the right kind of crimp beads to secure the wire. I recommend that you always test your crimp beads on the wire you've chosen before you begin a project, using the crimp bead size the wire manufacturer suggests. It's much better to discover you need to use a different crimp bead during a test than after your assembled piece has come undone . . . just ask Candace (one of my project testers)!

of strands, these wires come in different widths, the diameters of which are measured in decimal inches. The smallest wire I use is .010 inch (.25 mm) and the largest is .018 inch (.46 mm). When cutting wire, use toenail clippers or a cutter specifically designed for this type of wire. Don't use scissors or your best wire cutters to cut flexible beading wire, because the steel will ruin the blades of your good tools.

Metal wire is available in a wide variety of metal types, hardnesses, gauges, and profiles. It's used in this book primarily for creating jump rings (see Making Jump Rings, page 21), but also for creating bead dangles and links. Since wire becomes harder the more you manipulate it, *dead soft wire* is a good choice for making jump rings, a technique in which you want the wire to remain malleable throughout the several steps required. *Half-hard wire* is perfect for forming simple- or wrapped-loop links; the wire isn't manipulated as much, but it needs to keep its shape. The projects in this book were made with wire measured according to American Wire Gauge (AWG) standards, also known as Brown & Sharpe. Imperial Standard Wire Gauge (SWG) is the British standard used for measuring the diameter of wire. This gauge measurement is based on the metric system, so perfectly converting from AWG to SWG is impossible. For success with the projects in this book, be sure to use rings and wire that are measured with AWG standards. The larger the gauge measurement, the thicker the wire.

Tools

You'll use quite an assortment of tools to create the projects in beadmaille. Because it's a combination of bead weaving and chainmail, you'll use the tools typically used for both. Here you'll find a listing of the tools used for the projects in this book as well as some additional tools you'll need for making your own jump rings.

Beading awls are very thin, sharp-ended tools that are indispensable for loosening knots in thread. Just stick the tip of the tool into the center of the knot, then push the knot down the awl's slightly tapered shaft. This will open up the knot enough for you to untie it. Awls are also great to pick out the thread when you have to rip out a mistake. Use an awl for these jobs and your needles will thank you!

Beading needles are specialized needles that are longer and have smaller eyes than other needles. Most of the projects in this book use needles from size 10 (the largest), to size 13 (the smallest).

Scissors are a necessity for any type of beadwork. I like to use sharp embroidery scissors for cutting thread off the spool.

Thread burners are battery-operated tools with a tiny pointed wire at the tip that heats up to burn thread with pinpoint precision. Thread burners make it easy to trim thread close to the beadwork, and since synthetic thread ends shrink back into the beads after you melt them, it makes for an especially clean cut. Because the little ball of melted thread is difficult to feed through the eye of a needle, I only use the thread burner to trim thread tails.

Round-nose pliers have rounded, tapered tips that are useful for making wire loops. The size of the loop is determined by where you grip the wire on the pliers.

Notched flat-nose pliers narrow right at the tip. The result is a very small, thin, yet strong pair of pliers that can fit in the tightest of places.

Chain-nose pliers taper down to a point at the end and have a rounded backside. Never substitute needle-nose pliers or any other pliers with teeth when making jewelry as they will mar your wire.

Flat-nose pliers have wide, flat edges at the tip. Because they have more surface area, they are good for gripping while opening and closing jump rings.

Bent chain-nose pliers have tips that are similar to regular chain-nose pliers, but are bent at an angle. I like to use two of these to open and close my rings because it prevents my knuckles from knocking into each other. They also support the rings so they don't become distorted as you're working with them.

Crimping pliers are used for connecting 2 x 2-mm crimp tubes to flexible beading wire. They give a more refined look than simply collapsing the tubes with chain-nose pliers, but they can be tricky to use in certain beadmaille projects because it can be difficult to maneuver them without cracking a bead. *Micro crimping pliers* are specifically designed for 1 x 1-mm crimp tubes. A third type of crimping tool, *magical crimping pliers*, turn 2 x 2-mm crimp tubes into what appears to be a round bead. You must use the appropriately sized crimp bead and wire with this type of pliers for the crimp

to hold properly. This type of crimping can be hard to do in tight places, so save it for highly visible crimps. See Crimping, page 17 to learn how to use these pliers.

Wire cutters have pointed tips and sharp blades meant for cutting wire. They are especially important in beadmaille for making jump rings; the right cutter can really cut down on the work. Each type of cutter leaves a different kind of mark or *burr*, the smaller the better.

Ultra-flush or *razor-flush cutters* leave both wire ends nearly perfect and eliminate the need to flip the pliers. The downside to razor-flush cutters is the size of wire they can accommodate. The smoothest cutters typically can't cut anything much wider than 18-gauge wire.

Flush cutters leave one side of a wire cut smooth and the other side with a small pinch. If you use flush cutters for making jump rings, be sure to flip the cutters after every jump ring to snip off the burr from the previous cut.

Tools for Making Jump Rings

As you explore beadmaille, you will likely find how convenient it is to make your own jump rings. Here is a list of the tools you'll need:

Jeweler's saws are made up of a small frame that holds a very thin blade. They work great for quickly cutting wire coils into jump rings. If you use this technique, make sure the coil is clamped into a vise while cutting.

Cut lubricant is used to lubricate a wire coil created for jump rings, facilitating cutting and helping maintain the life of the jeweler's saw blade.

Metal needle files are used for removing rough spots or burrs from hand-cut jump rings, allowing them to close properly.

Jump ring-cutting attachments for a flex shaft tool are the most accurate and efficient way to cut your own jump rings. If you find yourself doing a lot of chainmail, I highly recommend getting one. My tool for cutting jump rings consists of a blade and a blade guard that fit over a coil holder (see below) to cut an entire wire coil in one movement. It enables you to wind and cut beautiful and accurate rings in minutes.

Mandrels are basically anything you use to wind wire around. There are precisely tooled steel rods made for this purpose, but you can also use anything from a knitting needle to the body of a permanent marker.

Wooden dowels are round pieces of wood that you insert into a wire coil before cutting the coil into jump rings with a jeweler's saw or flex shaft tool. Have lots of sizes on hand.

Winders are tools used for quickly and efficiently making coils for handmade jump rings. They have an adjustable chuck that accepts 1.5- to 12-mm mandrels, and a handle for winding the perfect coil.

Coil holders do just what it says: lock a wire coil in place. The tool's lid has a slot that guides the saw blade as you cut jump rings with a flex shaft tool.

Other Tools You May Need

Here are a few more tools that may be useful in making jump rings or for your other jewelry-making endeavors:

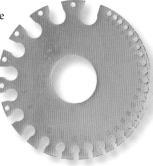

Wire gauge tools help you quickly identify the gauge of an unidentified piece of wire or stray jump ring. Simply see which is the smallest slot (not hole!) the wire will slide into.

Calipers are jawed tools that measure anything from a wire's diameter to the size of a mandrel or bead.

Rotary tumblers are small machines you fill with *stainless steel shot* and a *burnishing compound* in order to work harden and shine metal. They are useful if you make your own jump rings. Note: Don't attempt to tumble finished beadmaille jewelry in a tumbler—the glass beads will easily break.

Polishing pads are 2-inch (5.2 cm) foam squares that have micro-abrasives permanently bonded to them, making it easy to shine metals. These are fairly new on the market and just terrific. They work well for touch-ups and don't leave any residue on your hands. You can also use a *polishing cloth* for this purpose. Look for a type with a polishing compound built in so all you have to do is rub the metal a bit to achieve a nice bright shine.

Anti-tarnish storage is essential to keep your pieces looking good. I like to store my finished pieces in a plastic bag with a piece of anti-tarnish paper. Because the finished jewelry can be a little hard to polish, it's good to prevent oxidation before it starts. The paper lasts six to 12 months and works on silver, nickel, copper, bronze, brass, tin, and gold. You can also buy storage cases or jewelry boxes that have anti-tarnish fabric built in.

Techniques

Beadmaille truly is a hybrid of bead weaving and chainmail. You'll need to understand both techniques to create the projects in this book.

General Bead Weaving

Well-stitched beadwork is the key to creating secure and sturdy beadmaille. Learn the following terms and techniques common to all bead weaving stitches, and you'll be on your way to making great-looking projects.

Leaving a tail thread

Leave at least 6 to 8 inches (15.2 to 20.3 cm) of thread at the start of any bead-weaving project. This "tail" thread is woven back into the project when the piece is finished, further securing the beadwork.

Conditioning thread

Lay the thread across the thread conditioner and hold it down with your thumb. Pull the thread with the other hand. Make sure to pull upward against your thumb and not downward across the lip of the container, which would cause the thread to curl and become difficult to use.

Adding thread

You'll know it's time to add more thread when you have only 6 to 8 inches (15.2 to 20.3 cm) of thread left in your project. Leave the needle on but set the working thread aside. Cut a new piece of thread and place a needle on the end. Insert the new needle into the beadwork, following an existing thread path. Exit between two beads (figure 1). Pass under an existing thread and pull through until just a small loop remains. Pass the needle through the loop and tighten. This is called a *half-hitch knot* (figure 2). Pass through a few more

beads and tie another half-hitch knot. Repeat a few more times. Be sure the thread path changes direction so all the knots are not in a straight row (figure 3). Weave through the beadwork until the new thread exits from the same place as the old thread (figure 4). By leaving the old needle on, there will be no mistake about where you need to exit to continue in the proper place. Finish the old thread in the same way you started the new one, tying a few half-hitch knots between beads. Try to tie the knots in different places from where the new thread was tied.

Securing thread

To end a stitched project, tie half-hitch knots just like when you add thread. Make sure not to pull too tight when retracing the thread path. It will make your piece warp. Pass through another bead or two to hide the knots, pull the thread up and away from the beadwork, and trim the thread very close to the beadwork with a thread burner. Be careful with the thread burner so as to not cut through your entire piece!

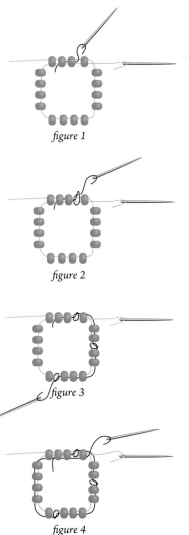

figure 1

figure 2

figure 3

figure 4

Bead Weaving Stitches

Beadmaille can be created with any number of techniques that involve using a needle and thread to stitch beads to one another, creating a sort of beaded fabric.

Right-angle weave

Right-angle weave is the stitch I use most often in the projects because it easily accommodates metal rings. There will be plenty of variations in the number of beads used for each wall, and how they are connected together, but each variation follows the same type of thread path. Right-angle weave is made up of a series of squares, or *units* of beads that all sit at right angles to one another. It can be a tough stitch to explain, so I like to use construction analogies to describe it to my students. It makes people laugh, but it is really helpful.

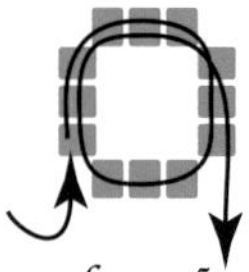

Imagine an apartment building. In cross section, it has a ceiling, a floor, and two walls. I call the wall between two apartments the "common wall." For this example, we will have a twelve-bead "apartment." Begin by picking up 12 beads. Pass through them all again and continue through the first nine beads strung (figure 5). The needle exits from the bottom of the first common wall, completing the first apartment (or unit).

Because the second apartment will be sharing the three beads of the common wall, you only need to pick up nine beads to make another apartment. Pass down through the top of the common wall (figure 6) and the first six beads just strung to exit from the top of the next common wall, completing the second apartment (figure 7). Pick up nine beads and pass up through the common wall (figure 8) and the first six beads just strung (figure 9). Continue in the same fashion. Notice that you'll be alternating between passing up through and down through the common wall with the addition of each apartment; don't worry or think too hard about where you are, just make sure you never enter the common wall where the thread is exiting (figure 10). (See the big red "X"!)

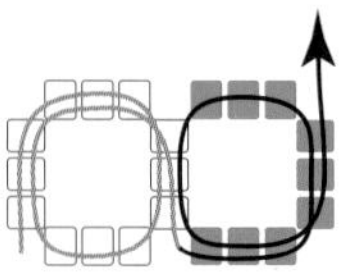

Double-needle right-angle weave

Some of the heavier projects in this book require flexible beading wire instead of thread. For those projects, you'll be working *double-needle right-angle weave*, a quick technique which doesn't really involve any needles at all! Projects will begin in the middle of a piece of wire. You add beads to each wire end, then you cross the wire ends through another bead or beads. This method keeps the beadwork very even and strong.

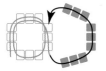
figure 5

figure 6

figure 7

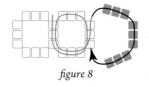
figure 8

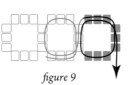
figure 9

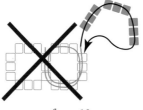
figure 10

Peyote stitch

The unique thing about peyote-stitched beads is the way they are transformed into a solid, flexible fabric. Peyote stitch begins by picking up a row of beads then turning the needle around in order to work back across the row. Pick up a bead, skip a bead, stitch through the next bead, and repeat the sequence. The result is a zigzag of beads that nest perfectly together like a brick wall (figure 11). The beads that stick out of each row are called *up beads*. As you continue to add rows, you'll pick up a bead, pass through the next up bead, and repeat. It's a really relaxing stitch because you don't have to think much or count. Triad Ring (page 69) and the Diamond Ring (page 117) both use peyote stitch to make nice smooth ring bands.

figure 11

Square stitch

Square stitch results in beads that sit in perfect rows and columns. Each bead is individually sewn to the one below it. Learn how to do this stitch as you create the giant bead rings in the Identical Triplets Necklace (page 84).

Crimping

Crimping is the best way to fasten off flexible beading wire. After stringing a piece, pick up a 2 x 2-mm crimp tube and the clasp. Pass the wire back through the crimp tube. Snug up the wire, making sure it's not twisted (figure 12). Place the crimp bead in the back groove of the crimping pliers. Squeeze the tube into a crescent shape (figure 13). Turn the crimp tube 90° and move it to the front notch of the pliers (figure 14). Squeeze again, forming the tube into a neat cylinder. Pull on the wire to make sure the crimp holds. *Note:* For smaller 1 x 1-mm crimp tubes, use micro crimping pliers.

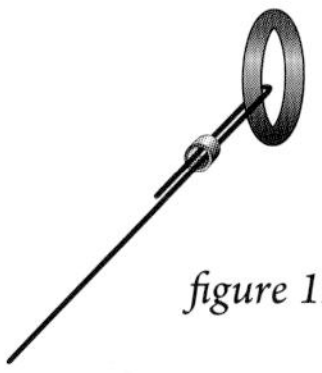

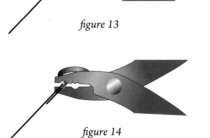

figure 12

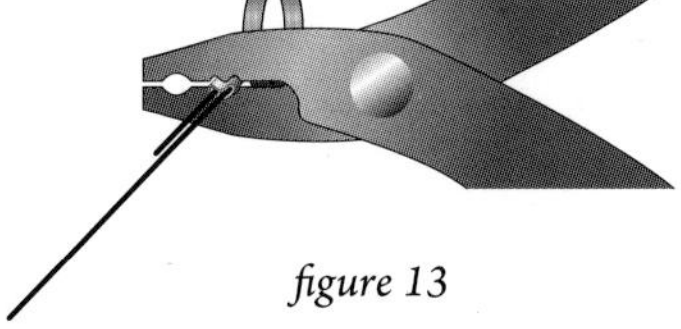

figure 13

figure 14

To transform a standard 2 x 2-mm crimp tube into what appears to be a nice, neat bead, use magical crimping pliers. Begin the crimp the same way you would with a regular crimp. Center the crimp bead over the dimple in the pliers. Squeeze gently but firmly to create a ravioli shape (figure 15). The tube will still move around, so hold it steady. Turn the tube 90° (figure 16) and squeeze again. Next, rotate the wire and crimp around as you open and close the pliers, shaping the tube into a round (figure 17). *Note:* This type of pliers is currently made for fine and heavy flexible beading wire only. You will also want to use only sterling silver or gold-filled crimp tubes because their soft and malleable bodies transform into a smooth finished product.

figure 15

figure 16

figure 17

You can also crimp by simply using chain-nose pliers to squeeze crimp beads or tubes onto the wire. Be sure the wires aren't crossed and are centered in the crimp bead. I suggest this simplified technique for several projects in this book because it is easy to do in the tight spaces between seed beads.

Wirework

You'll need a few basic wireworking skills to provide the finishing touches to some of the designs.

Simple loop

A simple loop produces just that—a simple loop at the end of a wire. This type of loop is typically used for making beaded links and can be opened and closed at will.

To make a simple loop, make sure the end of the wire is cut flush. Grip the wire in a pair of round-nose pliers such that the wire end is secure, but not protruding out of the pliers (figure 18). Roll the pliers forward until the end touches the straight wire. Remove the round-nose pliers. Use the tip of chain-nose pliers to grip the wire inside the loop so that it is even with the wire end (figure 19). Bend the loop back at a sharp 90° angle. Re-insert the round-nose pliers and bend the loop back up until it's perfectly centered over the wire, giving the appearance of a lollipop (figure 20). To make a beaded link, add a bead to the wire and form another simple loop as close as possible to the bead.

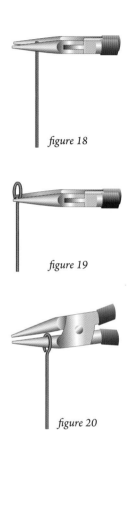

figure 18

figure 19

figure 20

Use a Light Touch

Crimping beadmaille requires delicate handling to prevent cracking a bead. No matter what type of crimp bead or pliers you use, follow the same precautions: Leaving the wires a bit loose, gently grip the crimp bead with the pliers. Snug up the wire, then crimp. This will help ensure that there are no beads in the pliers. If one sneaks in there, it will be smashed to bits . . . so be really careful!

figure 21

figure 22

Wrapped loop

A wrapped loop is a permanently closed loop at the end of a wire or headpin. After the loop is formed, the wire is wrapped around itself a few times for security. Begin by stringing beads onto a wire or headpin. Use the tip of chain-nose pliers to grip the wire that exits the last bead as close to the bead as possible (figure 21). Bend the wire at a 90° angle. Use round-nose pliers to grip the wire as close as possible to the bend (figure 22). Use your finger to push the wire end up and around the top jaw of the pliers. Reposition the pliers so that the bottom jaw is in the loop. Continue to push the wire around the jaw until it is back to its starting position (figure 23). Use flat-nose pliers to grasp the loop and chain-nose pliers to grasp the wire tail. Holding the loop securely, wrap the tail around the straight wire about two times (figure 24). Trim the tail wire close to the wrap with flush cutters.

figure 23

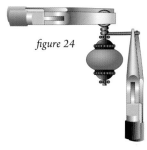

figure 24

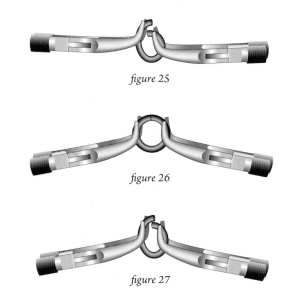

figure 25

figure 26

figure 27

Cautions for Adding Jump Rings to Beadwork

One of the trickiest aspects of assembling beadmaille is that you're working with tiny bits of glass, surrounded by moving metal rings. Glass beads will crack or break! You have to be very careful not to get a bead caught in the pliers. They will shatter in an instant.

Here's how to avoid that minor calamity. First, grip the right side of the ring close to the opening. Insert it into the beadwork then carefully grip the left side with another pair of pliers. Reposition the first pliers, making sure the beadwork is free. Begin closing the ring slowly. Listen for any crunching sounds. If a bead is caught, and you can hear it before if breaks, then reposition the pliers. Close the ring. Let go with the left pliers. Make sure it is closed well, then let go with the right pliers. By not letting go entirely the first time, you will speed things up because one pair of pliers is already in the right spot, and you are guaranteed that the beads are not caught.

Opening and closing rings

You'll need to open jump rings for beadmaille projects a bit wider than you might for traditional chainmail as the rings have to fit around beads as well as other rings. Open the rings consistently, with the right side toward you (figure 25).

To close jump rings, use two pairs of bent chain-nose pliers to grip each side. Wiggle the jump ring back and forth until the ends click closed (see the box on adding jump rings below). The ends should meet perfectly and the ring should remain round (figure 26).

Conditioning rings

Conditioning, or *work hardening*, jump rings is important to do before you use them in a project. Conditioning strengthens the jump rings, helping the wire keep its shape. Grip each side of the jump ring with a pair of bent chain-nose pliers (figure 27). Twist the jump ring back and forth a couple of times while gradually working the ends together until they click. This will begin hardening the ring at the point where it was twisted.

Making Jump Rings

You can easily and efficiently make your own jump rings for beadmaille projects. Making your own frees you to use any size ring in any wire gauge you choose—you aren't limited to what's available for purchase. I especially like the flexibility of choosing my metal color to complement my beads, something that's not always possible with commercial jump rings. My favorite jump ring metals are sterling silver, gold-filled, argentium sterling, copper, red brass, fine silver, and nickel wire. Many of these metals naturally patina or darken, so it's a good idea to factor in the wire's aged color as well, giving even more color options with which to design.

There are many ways to create your own rings. These methods range from using very simple to very specialized tools. All methods involve winding wire around a specifically sized cylinder into a coil, then cutting the coil into individual rings.

To make your own jump rings, first wrap the wire around a mandrel sized to produce your desired ring width. Form the same amount of wraps as you'd like rings, plus several more. Keep the coil as tight as possible, allowing each revolution to touch the previous one. Remove the coil from the mandrel and trim the ends. Note: If you're making hundreds of jump rings, you might like to use a winder (page 14) made just for this purpose. If you do use a winder, consider wearing a cotton glove to help reduce the friction between the wire and your thumb.

Next you cut the coils into rings. If you are making only a few rings, pull the coil apart slightly and flush cut the wire end (figure 28). Flip the flush cutters over and line it up with the cut you just made (figure 29). Cut, then flip the cutters over again and trim off the burr you just created. Repeat until all the rings are cut. Make sure each cut is straight and parallel. If there are visible burrs, use a metal needle file to smooth them.

If you're making more than a few rings, use a jeweler's saw or flex shaft jump ring cutter to cut the coils. For either type of tool, rub a generous amount of cut lubricant along the length of the coil; this will help preserve your blade. If you're using a jeweler's saw, use steady, even strokes to cut each ring off the coil. With a jump ring cutter, first insert a dowel that fills the coil. Lay the coil in a coil holder, pushing to the end closest to you. Tighten the plate until it's snug but not bowing. Carefully insert the jump ring cutter blade into the slot, start the motor at high speed, and pull the blade through the rings with a smooth, firm, downward motion. Let the blade stop spinning before you remove it. Open the coil holder and remove your fabulous rings.

Place the rings in a rotary tumbler (see page 14) to remove the excess lubricant, smooth any burrs, harden the rings, and make them shiny and smooth.

figure 28   *figure 29*

art deco necklace

Frame a lampworked focal bead with embellished chainmail arranged in fan patterns to create this sophisticated necklace.

Supplies

- Fine (.010–.012-inch [.25.–30 mm]) flexible beading wire, 6 feet (1.8 m)
- 1 copper wire protector, 4.6 x 4 mm (.56 mm I.D.)
- 1 copper button with shank, ³⁄₈-inch (9 mm)
- Matte metallic olive size 11° seed beads, 12 g
- 46 green jasper glass drop beads, 4 x 6 mm
- 2 copper Bali-style rondelle beads, 10 x 9 mm
- 2 copper Bali-style bead caps, 7 mm
- 1 multi-colored lampworked focal bead, 1¼-inch (3.2 cm)
- 2 copper or gold crimp tubes, 1 x 1 mm
- 92 copper 18-gauge open jump rings, 4.5 mm I.D.
- 276 copper 20-gauge open jump rings, 3 mm I.D.
- Wire cutters
- Various pliers

Techniques: Double-needle right-angle weave, chainmail variation

Finished size: 22 inches (55.9 cm)

Note: You may make adjustments to the necklace length by stitching the beaded portion a bit shorter than the desired length. Keep in mind that the finished piece will stretch one inch (2.5 cm) from the weight of the rings, so you'll need to plan accordingly.

1 Use the beading wire to string on the wire protector and the button. Slide the findings to the wire's center. Cross the wire ends through one seed bead (figure a).

a

2 Pick up seven seed beads on each wire. Cross the wire ends through one drop bead (figure b).

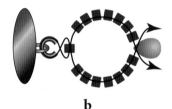

b

3 Repeat step 2 (figure c) until you've used a total of 23 drops.

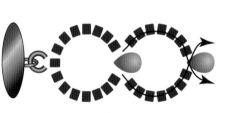

c

4 Pick up seven seed beads on each wire. Cross the wire ends through one seed bead (figure d).

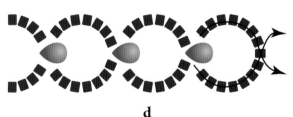

d

5 Gather the wire ends together and string on one rondelle, one bead cap from outside to inside, the focal bead, one bead cap from inside to outside, and one more rondelle. Separate the wire ends and cross them through one seed bead (figure e).

6 Repeat step 2 (as shown in figure f) and step 3.

7 Pick up seven seed beads on each wire. Cross the wire ends through one crimp bead (figure g). Pick up eight seed beads on each wire. Cross the wire ends through one crimp bead and the adjacent seed bead to form a loop (figure h). Check to see if the button fits snugly through the loop and make any necessary adjustments. Snug the beads, crimp the crimp beads, and trim the wire close to the work. Set the necklace aside.

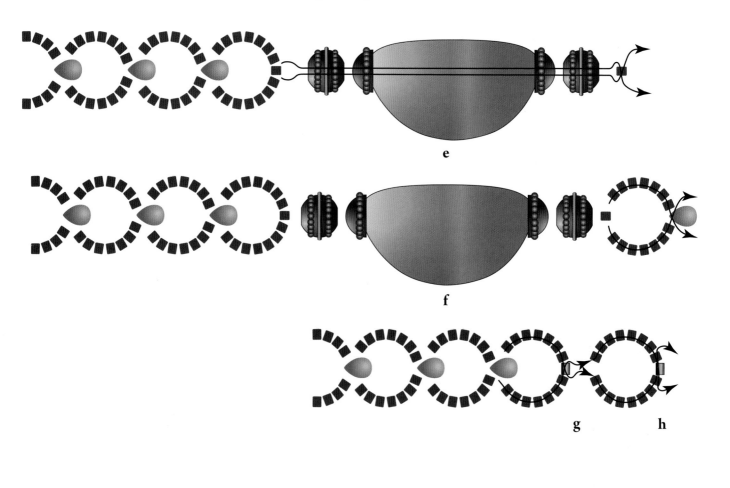

e

f

g   h

8 Open all the jump rings. Connect two 4.5-mm jump rings through neighboring beaded circles, one on each side of the drops (figure i).

9 Starting at the button end, use two 3-mm jump rings to connect each set of 4.5-mm jump rings placed in step 8 together (figure j). Stop when you reach the center of the necklace. Repeat from the other end (excluding the button loop), working toward the center so that the fan shapes mirror each other on each side of the necklace.

10 Connect two 3-mm jump rings to each side of the jump rings placed in step 9. Place the jump rings so that they loop around the edge of the beadwork and through the stacked 3-mm jump rings (figure k).

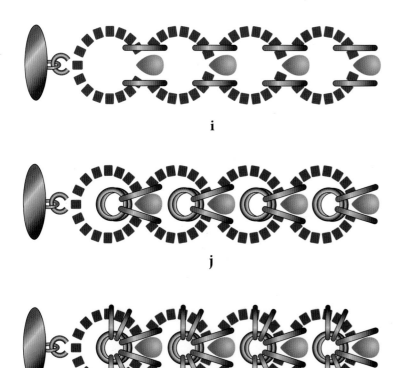

i

j

k

beadmaille necklace

This stately necklace of seed beads and decorative metal rings drapes and flows around the neck. You can familiarize yourself with this pattern by making the Accordion Cuff (page 42) first.

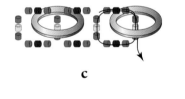

Supplies

Crystal 6-pound (2.7 k) braided beading thread

Size 11° seed beads:
   Silver-lined violet alabaster, 7 g (A)
   Frosted silver-lined clear, 3 g (B)
   Opaque indigo, 2 g (C)

61 silver hammered rings, 9 mm O.D.

1 silver hammered oval ring, 12 x 18 mm O.D.

1 silver wire protector, 4.6 x 4 mm (.56 mm I.D.)

1 silver hammered teardrop toggle clasp, 20 mm

Thread conditioner

Size 12 beading needle

Scissors

Thread burner

Techniques: Right-angle weave, European chainmail variation

Finished size: 18 inches (45.7 cm)

Side 1, row 1

1 Thread the needle with 4 yards (3.7 m) of conditioned thread. Pick up ABA, ACA, ABA, ACA, and one 9-mm ring. Pass through the first nine beads and ring to form a right-angle weave unit and capture the ring, leaving a 1-yard (.9 m) tail (figure a). The last three beads will be referred to as the "common wall." The working thread should exit the bottom of the common wall, below the ring.

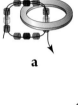

a

b

2 Pick up ACA, ABA, and ACA. Pass down through the common wall and the first six beads just strung to exit up through the second common wall (figure b). The two units will sit on either side of the ring.

c

3 Pick up ACA, ABA, ACA, and one 9-mm ring. Pass up through the common wall and the first six beads just strung (figure c). The working thread should exit the common wall below the ring.

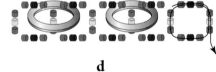

d

4 Repeat steps 2 and 3 to form a chain with a total of eighteen 9-mm rings. Repeat step 2 without any rings two times so that the chain has a total of 37 squares (figure d). The thread should exit down through the last common wall. Fold the last two units around the final ring added to change direction and set up row 2.

Side 1, row 2

Note: *The beaded chain section of the necklace is continuous and doesn't connect to the beads of the previous round, unless specified in the diagrams.*

5 Pick up ACA, ABA, ACA, and one 9-mm ring. Pass up through the final ring in row 1 and down through the common wall to capture both rings with the unit (figure e). Pass through the first six beads just strung, capturing both rings.

6 Pick up ACA, ABA, and ACA. Pass up through the common wall capturing both rings with a new unit and pass through the first six beads just strung.

7 Repeat steps 5 and 6 until there are seven rings in row 2.

8 Connect row 2 to row 1 as follows (figure f): Pick up ACA and pass up through the nearest row 1 common wall. Pick up ACA and pass down through the row 2 common wall. Weave through the row 2 beads to exit from the common wall between the fifth and sixth rings of row 2.

Side 1, row 3

9 Pick up ACA, ABA, and ACA (shown in pink, left side of figure g). Pass down through the common wall and the first six beads just strung.

10 Pick up ACA, ABA, and ACA. Pass down through the nearest ring from row 2 only (figure g) and pick up one 9-mm ring. Pass through the common wall and the first six beads just strung, making sure that the new ring is stacked below the previous row.

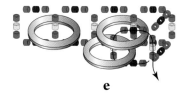

e

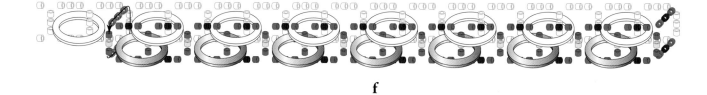

f

g

11 Repeat steps 9 and 10 until five rings have been added. Connect row 3 to row 2 by picking up ACA. Pass down through the nearest common wall in row 2. Pick up ACA and pass up through the nearest common wall in row 3 (pink beads at right, figure g).

Focal

12 Form a center common wall by working perpendicularly to the existing beadwork. Pick up AACAA, ABA, AACAA, and one 9-mm ring. Pass down through the common wall and the first eight beads just strung, capturing the ring around the common wall. Pick up ACA, ABA, and ACA. Pass up through the common wall and the first six beads just strung. Pick up ACA, ABA, ACA, and the 12 x 18-mm ring. Pass down through the common wall, capturing the ring (figure h). Repeat the thread path to reinforce the unit. Weave through the beads to exit from the center common wall of the first row.

Side 2, row 1

13 Repeat side 1, row 1, except begin with ACA, ABA, ACA, and a ring. Pass the needle down through the first existing common wall. Continue to mirror side 1, row 1. Repeat the thread path of the final unit to reinforce, except exit from the middle bead of the previous common wall.

14 Pick up one A, one wire protector, the clasp bar, and another A. Pass through the middle bead of the last common wall. Make sure to add the clasp so that it sits on the outside back of the unit (figure i). Repeat the thread path a few times to reinforce. Exit from the last common wall.

Side 2, row 2

15 Following the established bead color pattern, work a row of right-angle weave through the rings placed in side 2, row 1 for 22 units. Pick up ACA and pass through the nearest common wall in row 1. Pick up ACA and pass through the common wall to complete the unit. Work the remaining units with rings to add a total of seven rings to mirror side 1, row 2, making sure the rings stack the same way as side 1. Connect the final unit in this row to the center common wall of side 1, row 2: Pick up ACA, pass through the common wall at the center, pick up ACA, pass through the common wall inside both rings. Pass through the first three beads strung and the center common wall.

h

i

Side 2, row 3

16 Weave through the beads to exit from the center common wall of row 3. Stitch a matching five-ring row. Connect row 3 to row 2 as in step 11. Weave back through the beads to the center common wall. Weave back through the beads perpendicularly to the common wall in the middle of the 9-mm focal ring added in step 12.

17 Pick up AACAA, ABA, and AACAA. Pass through just the first ring of side 2, row 3, and back into the same common wall (figure j). Pass through the first three beads strung to exit from a C bead in the new diagonal wall. Pick up ABA and pass through the C bead on the back side of the same diagonal wall. Weave through the beads to exit from the center common wall and repeat this step on the side 1 diagonal wall. This will make independent support loops to hold the 9-mm focal ring in place. Secure the working thread and trim.

Side 1, clasp

18 Place a needle on the tail thread. Pick up ACA, ABA, and ACA, pass through the common wall, and through all nine beads just strung and AC of the common wall. Pick up ACA, AA, the clasp ring, AA, and ACA. Pass through the middle bead of the final common wall. Make sure to add the clasp so that it sits to the outside (back) of the unit (figure k). Weave through the final unit several times to reinforce. Exit the final common wall.

19 Following the established bead color pattern, work a row of right-angle weave through the rings placed in side 1, row 1 for 21 units. Pick up ACA and connect to the common wall at the end of the partial row created in steps 5 through 8. Pick up ACA and pass through the previous common wall to complete the final unit. Secure the tail thread and trim.

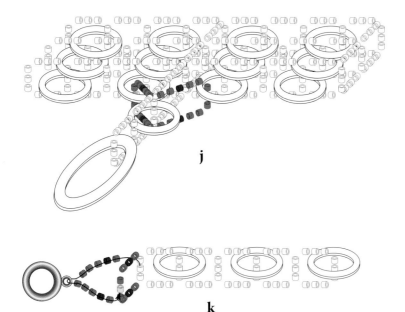

j

k

centipede bracelet

This beautiful design features a series of interlocking
jump rings and beads that skitter across your wrist
like a slinky, shiny centipede.

centipede bracelet

Supplies

Fine (.010–.012-inch [.25–.30 mm]) flexible beading wire, 4 feet (1.2 m)

Transparent topaz AB size 11° seed beads, 6 g

2 copper or gold crimp tubes, 1 x 1 mm

15 copper 14-gauge open jump rings, 8 mm I.D.

56 copper 14-gauge open jump rings, 5.5 mm I.D.

56 copper 16-gauge open jump rings, 3.5 mm I.D.

2 copper 16-gauge open jump rings, 5 mm I.D.

1 copper S-hook clasp, 18 mm

Wire cutters

Various pliers

Techniques: Double-needle right-angle weave, Celtic chainmail variation

Finished size: 7¾ inches (19.9 cm)

1 Cut 2 feet (61 cm) of flexible beading wire. Use the wire to pick up 20 beads. Slide the beads to the center of the wire, then cross the wire ends through the last bead strung to form the first unit (figure a).

2 Pick up nine beads on the left wire and nine beads on the right wire. Cross both wire ends through another bead (figure b). Repeat this step for a total of 13 units.

3 String nine beads on each wire. Cross both wire ends through one crimp tube. Pass each wire end through an adjacent seed bead (figure c). Snug the beads and use chain-nose pliers to crimp the tube. Trim any excess wire close to the beads.

4 Repeat steps 1 through 3 to make another strip of units. Stack the strips so that the units match. Set the strips aside.

5 Close all of the 8-mm jump rings. Condition and open all of the remaining jump rings. Set the rings aside.

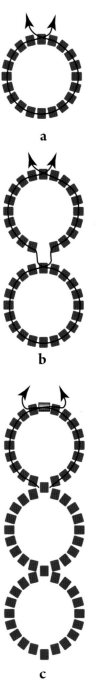

a

b

c

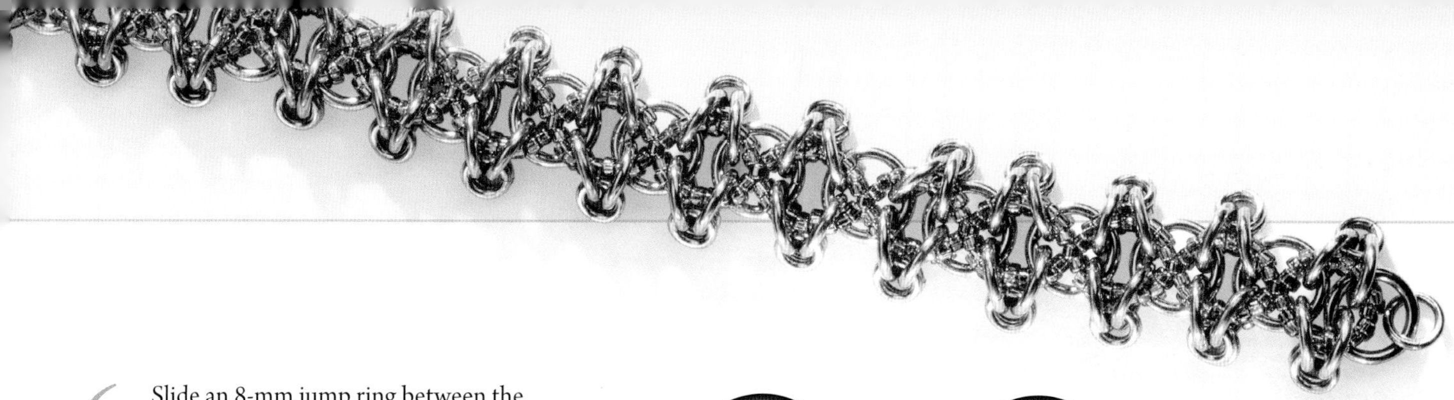

6 Slide an 8-mm jump ring between the strips so that half of it sticks out beyond the first set of units at one end of the strip. Attach a 5.5-mm jump ring to the left side of the strip, holding the 8-mm jump ring and the first set of units together. Repeat on the right side of the strip (figure d).

7 Slide another 8-mm jump ring between the strips so that it is centered between the first and second set of units. Attach a 5.5-mm jump ring to the left side of the strip, holding the 8-mm jump ring just placed and the first set of units together; repeat on the right side of the strip. Attach another 5.5-mm jump ring to the left side of the strip, holding the 8-mm jump ring just placed and the second set of units together; repeat on the right side of the strip (figure e). Continue in this fashion to the end of the strips, making sure that the last jump ring extends beyond the beaded strips as in step 6.

8 Starting at one end, connect each pair of 5.5-mm jump rings with pairs of 3.5-mm jump rings down both sides of the bracelet (figure f).

9 Use one 5-mm jump ring to attach one clasp half to each 8-mm jump ring on the ends of the bracelet (figure g).

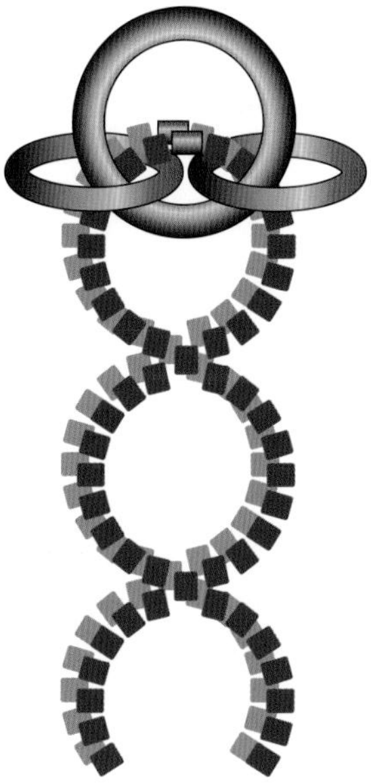

d

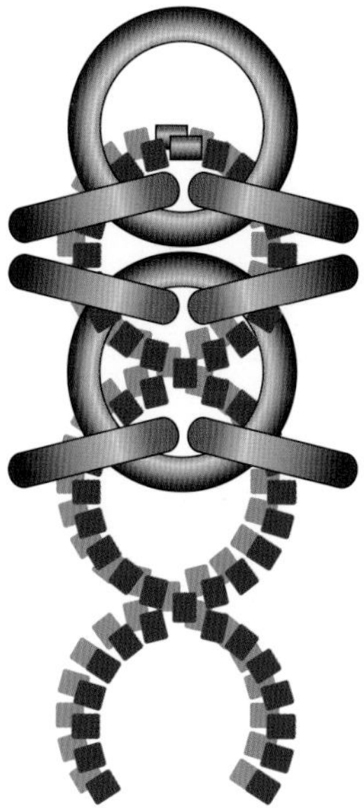

e

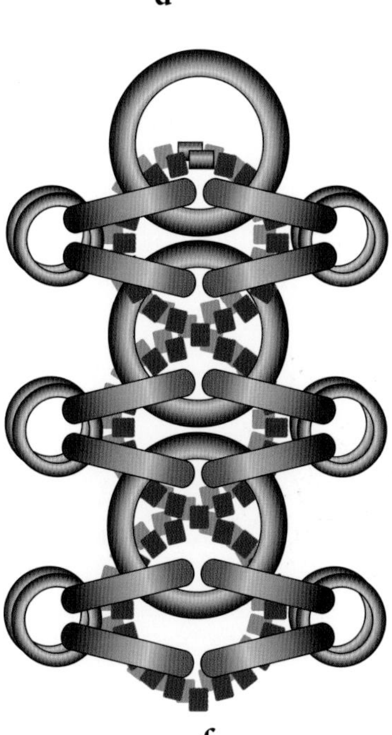

f

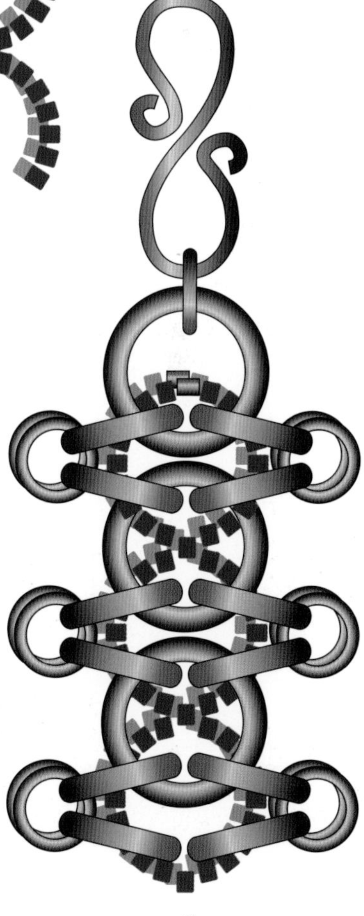

g

celtic lace necklace

This intricate necklace has its origins in Celtic chainmail, but it's transformed with seed beads. Luckily, the design is a snap to make.

Supplies

Fine (.010–.012-inch [.25–.30 mm])
flexible beading wire, 4 feet (1.2 m)

Celadon shimmer size 11° seed beads,
5 g

2 sterling silver crimp tubes, 1 x 1 mm

14 sterling silver 14-gauge open jump
rings, 8 mm I.D.

26 sterling silver 14-gauge open jump
rings, 5.5 mm I.D.

29 sterling silver 16-gauge open jump
rings, 3.5 mm I.D.

Heavy (.018–.019-inch [.46–.48 mm])
flexible beading wire, 2 feet (61 cm)

4 sterling silver crimp tubes, 2 x 2 mm

20 sterling silver bead caps, 5 mm

30 labradorite faceted rondelles,
5 x 8 mm

8 lemon jade round beads, 10 mm

2 sterling silver wire protectors,
4.6 x 4mm (.56 mm I.D.)

1 sterling silver filigree box clasp, 12 mm

1 sterling silver pinch bail to fit focal
bead, 10 mm

1 labradorite marquis cut focal bead,
10 x 25 mm

Wire cutters

Various pliers

Techniques: Double needle right-angle
weave, Celtic chainmail variation

Finished size: 19 inches (48.3 cm)

1   Cut 2 feet (61 cm) of fine flexible beading wire. Use the wire to pick up 20 seed beads. Slide the seed beads to the center of the wire and cross the wire ends through the last bead strung to form the first unit (figure a).

2   Pick up nine seed beads on the left wire and nine seed beads on the right wire. Cross the wire ends through another seed bead (figure b). Repeat this step for a total of 12 units.

3   Pick up nine seed beads on each wire. Cross both wire ends through a 1 x 1-mm crimp tube. Pass each wire end through an adjacent seed bead (figure c). Snug the beads and use chain-nose pliers to crimp the tube. Trim any excess wire close to the beads.

a

b

c

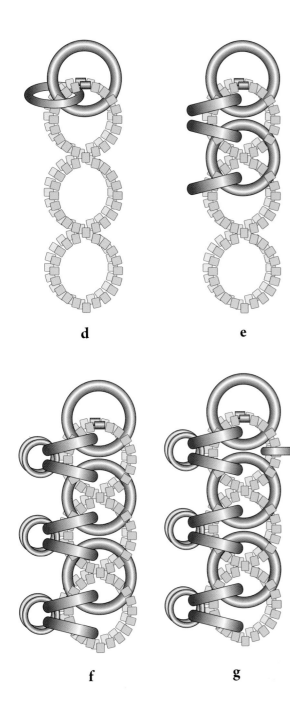

d

e

f

g

4 Repeat steps 1 through 3 to make another strip of units. Stack the strips so that the units match. Set the strips aside.

5 Close all of the 8-mm jump rings. Condition and open all the remaining jump rings. Set the rings aside.

6 Slide an 8-mm jump ring between the strips so that half of it sticks out beyond the first set of units at one end of the strip. Attach a 5.5-mm jump ring to the left side of the strip, holding the 8-mm jump ring and the first set of units together (figure d).

7 Slide another 8-mm jump ring between the strips so that it is centered between the first and second set of units. Attach a 5.5-mm jump ring to the left side of the strip, holding the 8-mm jump ring just placed and the first set of units together. Attach another 5.5-mm jump ring to the left side of the strip, holding the 8-mm jump ring just placed and the second set of units together (figure e). Continue in this fashion to the end of the strips, making sure that the last jump ring extends beyond the beaded strips as in step 6.

8 Starting at one end, connect each pair of 5.5-mm jump rings with pairs of 3.5-mm jump rings (figure f).

9 Attach one 3.5-mm jump ring to the right side of the first, center, and last sets of units to hold the beadwork together (figure g). Set the beadwork aside.

10 Cut 1 foot (30.5 cm) of heavy flexible beading wire; pick up one 2 x 2-mm crimp tube and eight seed beads. Pass the wire through one of the end 8-mm jump rings and back through the crimp tube, leaving a 1-inch (2.5 cm) wire tail (figure h). Snug the beads and use crimping pliers to crimp the tube.

h

variation

celtic lace necklace

i

j

11 Use the beading wire to string on one bead cap from outside to inside, three rondelles, one bead cap from inside to outside, and one 10-mm round bead (figure i); repeat three more times. Finish the strand with a bead cap/three rondelles/bead cap set to add a total of five rondelle sets and four 10-mm round beads. Pick up one 2 x 2-mm crimp tube, one side of the wire protector, and one half of the clasp. Pass back through the other side of the wire protector and the crimp bead (figure j). Snug the beads and use crimping pliers to crimp the tube. Trim any excess wire.

12 Repeat steps 10 and 11 on the other end of the strip to complete the other side of the necklace.

13 Attach the bail to the focal bead. Orient the necklace so that the 3.5-mm jump rings point down. Open one of the 3.5-mm jump rings at the center bottom of the necklace, slide on the bail, and close the jump ring. Note: If the bail won't fit onto the 3.5-mm jump ring, attach it to a thinner jump ring and connect it between the two centermost 3.5-mm jump rings.

caterpillar bracelet

This simple bracelet combines jump rings and
seed beads to create a chain that resembles a
plump mechanical caterpillar.

caterpillar bracelet

Supplies

Smoke 6-pound (2.7 k) braided
  beading thread

Size 11° seed beads
  Silver-lined lichen, 3 g (A)
  Matte metallic sage green, 3 g (B)

150+ copper 18-gauge open jump
  rings, 4 mm I.D.

1 copper toggle clasp, 12 mm

Thread conditioner

Size 10 beading needle

Scissors

Thread burner

Various pliers

Techniques: Right-angle weave,
  Japanese 8-4 chainmail variation

Finished size: 7 inches
  (17.8 cm)

1 Thread the needle with 2 yards (1.8 m) of conditioned thread. Pick up 10 beads, alternating A and B. Pass back through all the beads to form a right-angle weave unit. Pass through the first six beads strung, leaving a 6-inch (15.2 cm) tail (figure a). The last bead exited will be referred to as the "connecting bead."

2 Pick up nine beads, alternating colors starting with A. Pass though the connecting bead and the first five beads just strung (figure b).

3 Pick up nine beads, alternating colors starting with B. Pass through the previous connecting bead and the first five beads just strung (figure c).

4 Repeat steps 2 and 3 until you reach 1 inch (2.5 cm) shorter than the desired length, about 24 units. Don't trim the working thread. Move the needle to the tail; secure the tail thread and trim. Set the strip aside.

5 Repeat steps 1 through 4 to form a second strip.

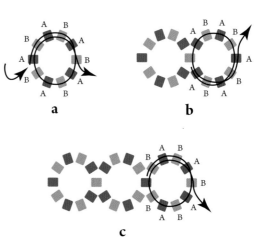

a

b

c

6 Stack the strips so the units match and the working threads are at the same end. Use two jump rings to connect the paired units (figure d) all the way down the strips. Open the strips so they lay flat (figure e).

7 Use two jump rings to connect neighboring units on the same strip (figure f). Repeat along the full length of both strips. Two pairs of rings will share the same unit. Connect two jump rings to each unit at the ends of the bracelet (figure g).

8 Use two jump rings to connect the four jump rings at one end of the bracelet (figure h). Use one jump ring to connect one half of the clasp to the two jump rings just placed (figure i).

9 Check the bracelet for fit. Make any adjustments to the beading at the other end of the bracelet; secure the thread and trim. Add or remove jump rings as necessary following step 7; finish as in step 8 using the second clasp half.

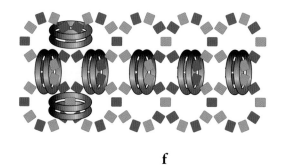

d

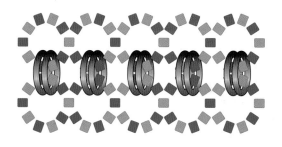

e

f

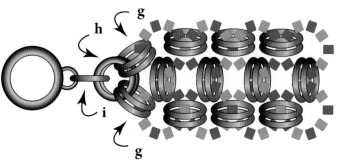

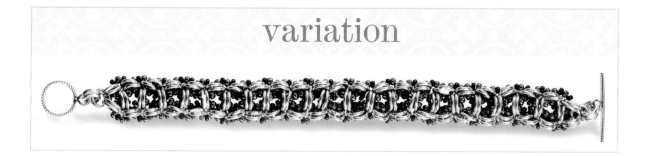

variation

accordion cuff

Right-angle weave layers slide freely back and forth
through decorative rings, while the gradated hues create
an exciting combination of color and movement.

Supplies

Smoke 6-pound (2.7 k)
braided beading thread

Size 11° seed beads:

Garnet/gold luster, 2 g (A)

Gold-lined cranberry, 2 g (B)

Silver-lined topaz rainbow, 2 g (C)

Dusty rose-lined amber, 2 g (D)

Matte transparent medium
amethyst, 2 g (E)

Purple-lined light topaz, 2 g (F)

Brown-lined blue, 2 g (G)

Silver-lined light amethyst AB,
2 g (H)

Gold luster light lavender, 2 g (I)

Matte dark bronze, 2 g (J)

24 silver decorative rings, 9 mm O.D.

10 to 12 silver 18-gauge open jump
rings, 4 mm I.D.

1 silver five- or six-strand bar clasp,
1 inch (2.5 cm)

Thread conditioner

Size 10 beading needle

Scissors

Thread burner

Techniques: Right-angle weave,
European chainmail variation

Finished size: 7¼ inches (18.4 cm)

Note: You may add or remove rows to
change the bracelet's length by
¾ inch (1.9 cm) for each layer.

Layer 1

1 Thread the needle with one yard of conditioned
thread. Pick up beads in the following color order: AAAAAJAAAAA, AJA, AAAAAJAAAAA,
and AJA. Pick up one 9-mm ring. Pass through
all the beads again to form a right-angle weave
unit that captures the ring, leaving a 6-inch
(15.2 cm) tail. Pass through the first 25 beads
strung (figure a). The last 11 beads passed
through will be referred to as the "common
wall." The thread should exit the bottom of the
common wall, below the ring.

2 Pick up AJA, AAAAAJAAAAA, and AJA. Pass
down through the common wall, capturing the
ring placed in the previous step, and through
the first 14 beads just strung to exit up through
the second common wall (figure b).

3 Pick up AJA, AAAAAJAAAAA, AJA, and one
9-mm ring. Pass up through the common wall
and through the first 14 beads just strung, capturing the new ring within the unit (figure c).

4 Repeat steps 2 and 3 until there is a total of
three rings in the chain. Repeat step 2. Weave
through the final unit again to reinforce; secure
the thread and trim. Place the needle on the tail
thread. Weave through the first unit to reinforce; secure the thread and trim. Set this aside.

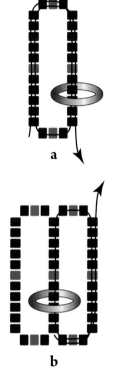

a

b

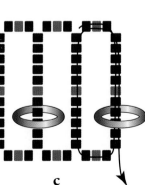

c

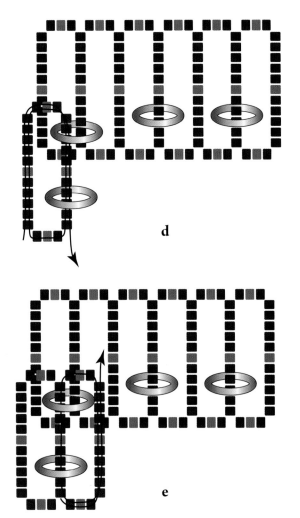

d

Layer 2

5 Thread the needle with one yard of conditioned thread. Pick up beads in the following color order: BBBBBJBBBBB, BJB, BBBBBJBBBBB, and BJB. Pass through the first ring from the previous row and pick up one 9-mm ring. Make sure the tail thread is to the outside left. Pass through all the beads and the new ring just strung to form a right-angle weave unit that captures the new ring, leaving a 6-inch (15.2 cm) tail. Pass through the first 25 beads just strung (figure d). As before, the last 11 beads will be referred to as the "common wall."

6 Pick up BJB, BBBBBJBBBBB, and BJB. Pass down through the common wall, capturing two rings. Pass through the first 14 beads just strung to exit up through the second common wall in this layer (figure e).

7 Pick up BJB, BBBBBJBBBBB, and BJB. Pass down through the second ring from the previous layer and pick up one 9-mm ring. Pass up through the common wall and the first 14 beads just strung, capturing two rings (figure f).

e

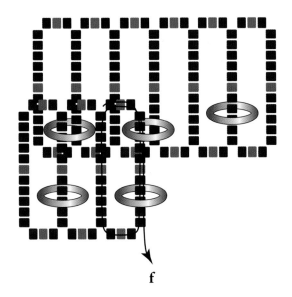

f

8 Repeat steps 6 and 7 until there is a total of three rings in the chain. Repeat step 6. Weave through the final unit again to reinforce; secure the thread and trim. Place the needle on the tail thread. Weave through the first unit to reinforce; secure the thread and trim.

Layers 3 through 8

9 Repeat layer 2, switching B for C, C for D, etc., until you've stitched a total of eight layers. Check that each layer stacks on top of the previous one like stair steps (figure g).

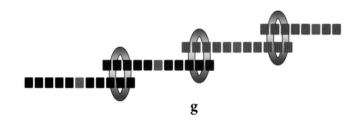

g

Layer 9

10 Repeat layer 2 without adding any new rings, but incorporating the rings from the previous layer (layer 8) as before.

11 Use jump rings to attach each clasp half to the beadwork at each end of the bracelet.

variation

This variation is made with seven layers and a 1-inch (2.5 cm) five-strand connector with a box clasp.

clover leaf ensemble

Weave seed beads and rings together,
forming cloverleaf patterns for a jewelry
set worthy of a Celtic queen.

Supplies

Grey size D nylon beading thread

Gold-lined ice blue size 11° seed
beads, 4 g

18 copper decorative rings, 9 mm
O.D.

4 copper 20-gauge open jump rings,
3 mm I.D.

2 copper ear wires

1 copper decorative oval ring,
7 x 13 mm O.D.

Fine (.010–.012-inch [.25–.30 mm])
flexible beading wire, 3 feet
(.9 m)

12 copper crimp tubes,
1 x 1 mm

1 copper toggle clasp, 12 mm

Copper-lined crystal size 15°
cylinder beads, 5 g

Thread conditioner

Size 13 beading needle

Scissors

Thread burner

Various pliers

Techniques: Right-angle weave,
chainmail variation

Finished size: Earrings: 1½ inches
(3.8 cm); Bracelet: 7 inches
(17.8 cm)

The bracelet should be worn snug.

Making the earrings

1 Thread the needle with 3 feet (.9 m)
of conditioned thread. Pick up 10 seed
beads and one 9-mm ring. Pass through
the beads again to form a unit and
capture the ring, leaving a 6-inch (15.2
cm) tail. Pass through the first seven
beads strung (figure a). The last two
beads exited will be referred to as the
"common wall."

a

2 Pick up eight seed beads. Pass down
through the common wall and the first
five beads just strung (figure b). The
two units will sit on either side of the
ring.

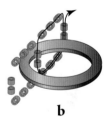

b

3 Pick up 10 seed beads. Pass up through
the common wall and the first six beads
just added (figure c).

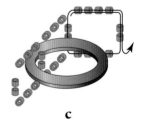

c

4 Pick up eight seed beads. Pass up
through the ring placed in step 1, pick
up one new ring, pass down through
the common wall, and through the first
five beads just added to capture both
rings with the unit (figure d).

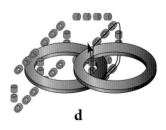

d

clover leaf ensemble

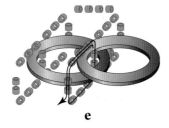

e

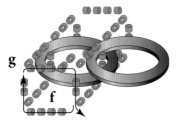

g **f**

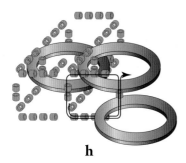

h

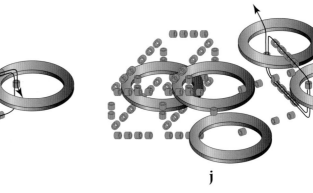

i **j**

5 Pick up eight seed beads. Pass up through the common wall, capturing both rings with a new unit, and through the first five beads just added (figure e).

6 Pick up four seed beads. Pass up through the common wall of the first unit added in step 1 (figure f). Pick up four seed beads. Pass down through the last common wall to finish the unit (figure g). Repeat the thread path to reinforce the unit, exiting down through the last common wall.

7 Pick up nine seed beads and one 9-mm ring. Pass down through the common wall and through the first five beads just added, capturing the ring just strung (figure h). The common wall is now only one bead.

8 Pick up nine seed beads and one 9-mm ring. Pass up through the common wall, capturing the previous ring, and through the first five beads just added, capturing the ring just strung between the last two units (figure i).

9 Pick up nine seed beads and one 9-mm ring. Pass down through the previous ring, the common wall, and through the first five beads just added, capturing the ring just strung (figure j).

10 Pick up four seed beads. Pass down through the common wall between the third and fourth units (figure k). Pick up four seed beads. Pass up through the last common wall to finish the unit (figure l). Repeat the thread path to reinforce the unit.

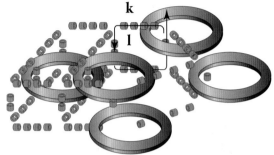

11 Weave through the beadwork to exit up through the common wall that runs through the first two rings placed. Pick up two seed beads and pass down through the common wall between the first two units (figure m). Pick up two seed beads and pass up through the common wall that runs through the first two rings placed (figure n). Because there are only two beads used, the stitch will pull the bottom set of units up at an angle (see photo). Secure the thread and trim.

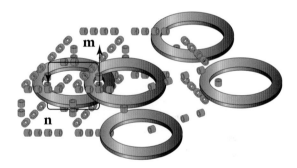

12 Connect one 3-mm jump ring to the first ring placed. Use one 3-mm jump ring to connect the last jump ring added to one ear wire (figure o).

13 Repeat steps 1 through 12 to make the matching earring.

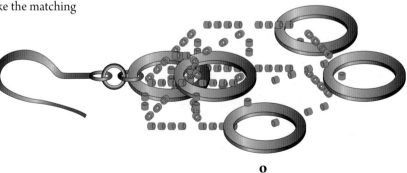

o

clover leaf ensemble

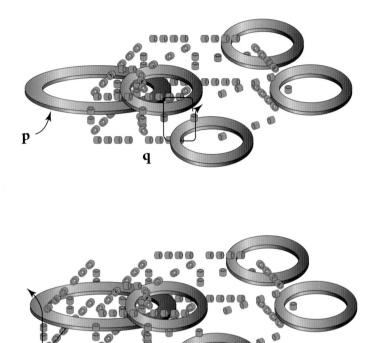

p

q

r

Making the bracelet

1. Repeat the earrings instructions, steps 1 through 11, to form the first side of the bracelet with these exceptions: Use 2 yards (1.8 m) of thread, and leave a 1 yard (.9 m) tail. Substitute the 7 x 13-mm oval for the first ring (figure p); after steps 7 and 10, pass through the beadwork to add one extra seed bead to act as a common wall holding the side rings in position to the outside (shown in pink, figure q); and at the end of step 11, repeat the thread path for all the beadwork until the beads are full. Secure the thread and trim.

2. Repeat the previous step using the tail thread, but incorporate the 7 x 13-mm oval ring already placed as the first ring. The second side will share the first two walls made (figure r). This will create a mirror image, centering both sides of the bracelet's focal piece around the oval (see photo). Make sure that the ring added in step 4 stacks the same way it did on the first side. Set the focal piece aside.

3. Cut an 8-inch (20.3 cm) piece of beading wire. Use the wire to string on one crimp tube and one half of the clasp. Pass back through the tube, leaving a 1-inch (2.5 cm) tail. Crimp the tube and trim the wire tail. String on one seed bead and six cylinder beads; repeat to form a strand 2 inches (5.1 cm) long, ending with cylinder beads (figure s).

variation

4 String on one crimp tube and seven seed beads.

5 Pass the wire through one of the focal piece's end rings and back through the crimp tube (figure t). Pull the wire snug and crimp the tube; do not trim the wire tail.

6 String on six cylinder beads and one seed bead; repeat to form a strand 2 inches (5.1 cm) long, ending with a seed bead. String on one crimp tube (figure u). Pass the wire through the clasp half, and back through the crimp tube and the next bead on the strand. Pull the beads snug, crimp the tube, and trim the wire tail.

7 Repeat step 3, connecting to the same clasp half. Pass through the same seven seed beads added in step 4. Repeat steps 5 and 6.

8 Repeat steps 3 through 7 to form the other side of the bracelet, connecting to the end ring on the other side of the focal piece and using the other clasp half.

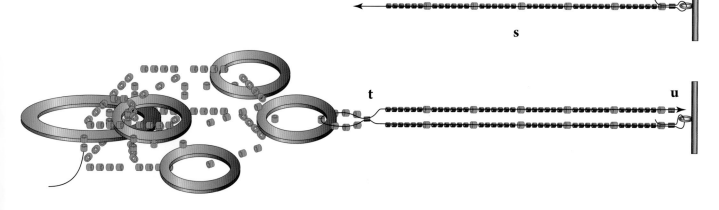

Layer a Celtic chainmail pattern with right-angle weave into a floral motif. You can use the pattern alone to create these dainty earrings, or multiply and link it into a graceful garland bracelet.

Bracelet Supplies

Fine (.010 or .012-inch [.25 or .30 mm]) flexible beading wire, 6 feet (1.8 m)

Matte transparent raspberry size 15° seed beads, 6 g

12 sterling silver crimp tubes, 1 x 1 mm

60 sterling silver 18-gauge open jump rings, 5.5 mm I.D.

76 sterling silver 20-gauge open jump rings, 4 mm I.D.

Sterling silver 20-gauge half-hard round wire, 1 foot (30.5 cm)

2 tourmaline 8 x 6-mm rondelles

1 sterling silver S-hook clasp, 18 mm

Wire cutters

Micro crimping pliers (optional)

Various pliers

Finished size: 7 inches (17.8 cm)

Techniques: Right-angle weave, Celtic chainmail variation

Making the bracelet

1 Cut a 12-inch (30.5-cm) piece of beading wire. Pick up 18 beads and slide them to the center of the wire. Pass through the first bead strung to form the first unit (figure a).

2 Pick up six beads on the left wire and 11 beads on the right wire. Cross the left wire through the last bead on the right wire (figure b).

3 Repeat step 2 twice to form a total of four units.

4 Pick up five beads and a crimp tube on the left wire and nine beads and a crimp tube on the right wire. Cross both wires through the seventh bead added to the first unit. Pass each wire through its adjacent crimp tube and the next seed bead (figure c). Pull the wires snug and crimp the tubes. Use wire cutters to trim the excess wire close to the beads. Set the flower aside.

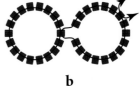

a

b

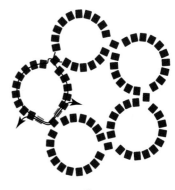

c

cherry blossom ensemble

d

e

f

5 Close all of the 5.5-mm jump rings; set them aside. Condition and open all of the 4-mm jump rings; set them aside as well.

6 Set one closed 5.5-mm jump ring on top of the flower at a point where two units intersect; set another 5.5-mm jump ring on the back of the flower so that the two jump rings sandwich the beadwork. Repeat to add two closed 5.5-mm jump rings to the next unit intersection. Use a 4-mm jump ring to connect all four 5.5-mm jump rings (figure d). Note: The 4-mm jump rings should connect the 5.5-mm jump rings only, not the beadwork. Sandwich the beadwork with two more 5.5-mm jump rings at the next unit intersection; use one 4-mm jump ring to connect these jump rings to the adjacent 5.5-mm jump rings. Repeat to add a total of ten 5.5-mm jump rings connected by five 4-mm jump rings around the flower (figure e).

7 Attach one more 4-mm jump ring to each of the 5.5-mm jump ring connections. These jump rings will sit parallel to the 4-mm jump rings placed in step 6 (figure f). Set the flower aside.

8 Repeat steps 1 through 7 to create a total of six flowers.

9 Set two flowers side by side so that two units of each flower touch. Use two pairs of 4-mm jump rings to connect the two flowers through the 5.5-mm jump rings (figure g). Set the component aside.

10 Repeat step 9 twice.

11 Cut the 20-gauge half-hard round wire into two 6-inch (15.2-cm) pieces.

12 Form a wrapped loop at the end of one wire that attaches to a pair of jump rings at one end of a component. String on one rondelle and form another wrapped loop that attaches to one end of a second component (figure h).

13 Repeat step 12 to connect the second component to the third.

14 Attach two 4-mm jump rings to the 5.5-mm jump rings at one end of the bracelet (figure i). Use two 4-mm jump rings to connect the clasp to the other end of the bracelet (figure j). Note: If desired, make a longer bracelet by adding beaded wrapped-loop links to each end of the bracelet before you add the clasp. Once the end links are placed, simply connect the clasp to a wrapped loop at one end of the bracelet.

g

i

h

j

cherry blossom ensemble

Earring Supplies

Fine (.010 or .012-inch [.25 or .30 mm]) flexible beading wire, 2 feet (61 cm)

Matte transparent raspberry size 15° seed beads, 2 g

4 sterling silver crimp tubes, 1 x 1 mm

20 sterling silver 18-gauge open jump rings, 5.5 mm I.D.

28 sterling silver 20-gauge open jump rings, 4 mm I.D.

2 sterling silver ear wires

Wire cutters

Micro crimping pliers (optional)

Various pliers

Finished size: 1 inch (2.5 cm)

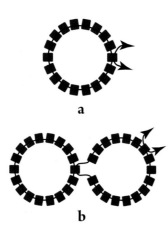

a

b

Making the earrings

1 Cut a 12-inch (30.5-cm) piece of beading wire. Pick up 18 beads and slide them to the center of the wire. Pass through the first bead strung to form the first unit (figure a).

2 Pick up six beads on the left wire and 11 beads on the right wire. Cross the left wire through the last bead on the right wire (figure b).

3 Repeat step 2 twice to form a total of four units.

4 Pick up five beads and a crimp tube on the left wire and nine beads and a crimp tube on the right wire. Cross both wires through the seventh bead added to the first unit. Pass each wire through its adjacent crimp tube and the next seed bead (figure c). Pull the wires snug and crimp the tubes. Use wire cutters to trim the excess wire close to the beads. Set the flower aside.

5 Close all of the 5.5-mm jump rings; set them aside. Condition and open all of the 4-mm jump rings; set them aside as well.

6 Set one closed 5.5-mm jump ring on top of the flower at a point where two units intersect; set another 5.5-mm jump ring on the back of the flower so that the two jump rings sandwich the beadwork. Repeat to add two closed 5.5-mm jump rings to the next unit intersection. Use a 4-mm jump ring to connect all four 5.5-mm jump rings (figure d). Note: The 4-mm jump rings should connect the 5.5-mm jump rings only, not the beadwork. Sandwich the beadwork with two more 5.5-mm jump rings at the next unit intersection; use one 4-mm jump ring to connect these jump rings to the adjacent 5.5-mm jump rings. Repeat to add a total of ten 5.5-mm jump rings connected by five 4-mm jump rings around the flower (figure e).

7 Attach one more 4-mm jump ring to each of the 5.5-mm jump ring connections. These jump rings will sit parallel to the 4-mm jump rings placed in step 6 (figure f).

8 Attach two 4-mm jump rings to one pair of 5.5-mm jump rings. Use two 4-mm jump rings to connect one ear wire to the pair of jump rings just added (figure g).

9 Repeat steps 1 through 8 to make the second earring.

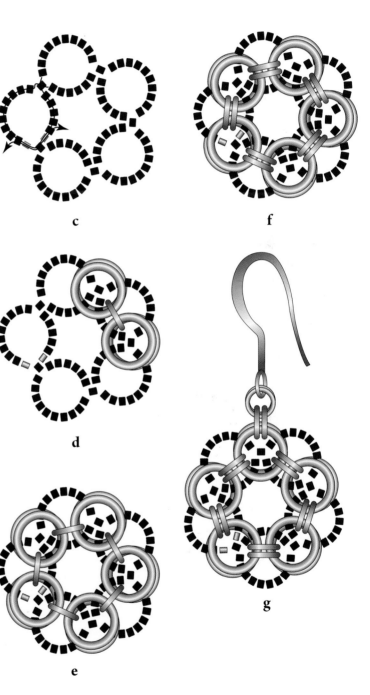

c

f

d

e

g

cleopatra necklace

This Egyptian-style collar is made thoroughly modern with the addition of rows of hammered metal rings interlaced with right-angle weave units.

Supplies

Teal D nylon beading thread

Size 11° seed beads:

Matte metallic patina iris, 16 g (A)

Gold-lined clear AB, 3 g (B)

Sand-lined clear, 3 g (C)

21 sterling silver decorative round rings, 13 mm O.D.

13 sterling silver decorative round rings, 9 mm O.D.

35 sterling silver decorative round rings, 18 mm O.D.

34 sterling silver 14-gauge open jump rings, 5.5 mm I.D.

1 sterling silver lobster clasp, 13 mm

Thread conditioner

Size 12 and 13 beading needles

Scissors

Thread burner

Various pliers

Techniques: Right-angle weave, European chainmail variation

Finished size: 19 inches (48.3 cm)

Note: The centerpiece construction is based on the London Flat Bracelet (page 88), so familiarize yourself first with its technique and instructions.

Middle row

1 Unspool and condition 2 yards (1.8 m) of thread. Don't cut the thread from the spool, as you'll use additional thread later to finish the second side of the row. Pick up 14 beads in this order: BAB, AAAA, BAB, and AAAA. Pick up one 13-mm ring, sliding the beads and ring to the spool. Pass through the first 10 beads, capturing the ring to form the first right-angle weave unit. The last three beads exited will be referred to as the "common wall." The thread should exit the bottom of the common wall, below the ring (figure a).

2 Pick up AAAA, BAB, and AAAA. Pass down through the common wall and continue through the first seven beads just added to exit up from the second unit's common wall. The two units will sit on either side of the ring (figure b).

3 Pick up AAAA, BAB, and AAAA. Pass up through the last common wall exited and continue through the first seven beads just added (figure c).

4 Pick up AAAA, BAB, AAAA, and one 13-mm ring. Pass down through the last common wall exited and continue through the first seven beads just added, capturing the ring around the common wall (figure d).

a

b

c

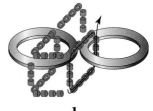

d

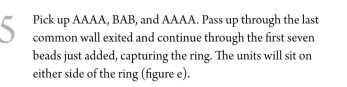

5 Pick up AAAA, BAB, and AAAA. Pass up through the last common wall exited and continue through the first seven beads just added, capturing the ring. The units will sit on either side of the ring (figure e).

6 Pick up AAAA. Pass up through the common wall of the first unit. Pick up AAAA. Pass down through the previous common wall to finish the unit (figure f).

7 Pick up AAAA, BAB, and AAAA. Pass down through the last common wall exited and continue through the first seven beads just strung (figure g).

8 Pick up AAAA, BAB, and AAAA. Pass down through the last ring placed. Pick up one 13-mm ring, then pass up through the last common wall exited, and continue through the first seven beads just added to capture both rings with the unit (figure h). Note: The first ring has just one common wall running through it, but all subsequent rings overlap and have two common walls going through them.

9 Pick up AAAA, BAB, and AAAA. Pass down through the last common wall exited, capturing both rings, and continue through the first seven beads just added (figure i).

10 Pick up AAAA. Pass down through the adjacent common wall on this side of the row. Pick up AAAA and pass up through the previous common wall to finish the unit (figure j).

e

f

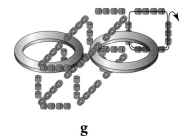

g

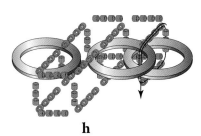

h

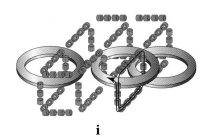

i

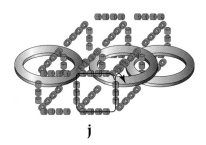

j

11 Pick up AAAA, BAB, and AAAA. Pass up through the last common wall exited and continue through the first seven beads just strung.

12 Pick up AAAA, BAB, AAAA, and one 13-mm ring. Pass up through the last ring placed, then pass up through the last common wall exited, and continue through the first seven beads just added to capture both rings with the unit.

13 Pick up AAAA, BAB, and AAAA. Pass up through the last common wall exited, capturing both rings, and continue through the first seven beads just added.

14 Pick up AAAA. Pass up through the adjacent common wall on this side of the row. Pick up AAAA and pass down through the previous common wall to finish the unit.

15 Repeat steps 7 through 14 to add a total of seven rings. Secure the working thread and trim.

16 Unspool and condition 2 more yards (1.8 m) of thread and cut. Move the needle to the tail. Rotate the piece 180° and pass up through the common wall so that the thread exits above the piece. Repeat steps 3 through 14, making sure the rings stack in a mirror image (figure k). Secure the thread and trim.

variation

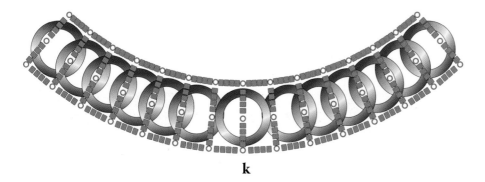

k

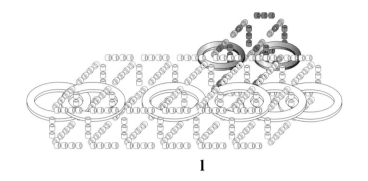

l

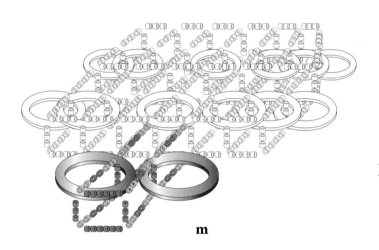

m

Top row

17 Unspool and condition 2 yards (1.8 m) of thread; don't cut the thread from the spool. Repeat steps 1 through 15, this time working off the common walls on one side of the center row. This row will also be different in that you'll use 9-mm rings, CAC for the vertical stitches, and AAA for the horizontal stitches. The common walls should remain BAB (figure l). Secure the working thread and trim.

18 Rotate the piece 180° and pass up through the common wall so the thread exits up through the common wall between the top and bottom rows. Unspool and condition 2 more yards (1.8 m) of thread and cut. Move the needle to the tail. Mirror the beadwork created in step 17, making sure the rings stack in a mirror image. Secure the thread and trim.

Bottom row

19 Unspool and condition 2 yards (1.8 m) of thread; don't cut the thread from the spool. Repeat steps 1 through 15, this time working off the common walls on the other side of the center row. This row will also be different in that you'll use 18-mm rings, CCAACC for the vertical stitches, and AAAAAA for the horizontal stitches. The common walls should remain BAB (figure m). Secure the working thread and trim.

20 Unspool and condition 2 more yards (1.8 m) of thread and cut. Move the needle to the tail. Make horizontal right-angle weave stitches between the first and second central common walls of each row as in figure f. This stitching will hold the center rings in place (figure n). For the bottom row use AAAAAA for the stitches, for the center row use AAAA, and for the top row use AAA.

21 Retrace the thread path back to the bottom row. Mirror the beadwork created in step 19, making sure the rings stack in a mirror image. Secure the thread and trim.

Assembly

22 Form a long chain section by connecting seven 18-mm rings, then four 13-mm rings, with 5.5-mm jump rings; set the chain aside. Form a short chain section by connecting four 18-mm rings with 5.5-mm jump rings; set the chain aside. Use one 5.5-mm jump ring to connect the last 9-mm ring at one end of the top row to the end 18-mm ring of the long chain section. Use one 5.5-mm jump ring to connect the last 18-mm ring of the bottom row to an end 18-mm ring of the short chain section. Use a 5.5-mm jump ring to connect the short chain section to the long chain section through the fourth 18-mm ring (figure o).

23 Repeat step 22 on the other side of the rows. Attach one 5.5-mm jump ring to the end 13-mm ring on one side of the necklace. Use a 5.5-mm jump ring to connect the clasp to the other end of the necklace.

o

n

Embellish a right-angle weave rope with intricate chainmail clusters, creating a slinky lariat necklace.

Supplies

Smoke 10-pound (4.5 k) braided beading thread

Size 11° seed beads:

Matte metallic patina iris, 6 g (A)

Matte metallic green iris, 6 g (B)

2 copper flower bead caps, 10 mm

2 copper daisy spacers, 4 mm

1 copper green lampworked focal bead, 15 x 20 mm

6 matte metallic green iris size 15° seed beads

1 transparent aqua Czech glass drop bead, 4 x 6 mm

168 copper 18-gauge open jump rings, 5 mm I.D.

84 copper 18-gauge open jump rings, 5.5 mm I.D.

84 copper 18-gauge open jump rings, 4 mm I.D.

Thread conditioner

Size 10 and 12 beading needles

Scissors

Thread burner

Various pliers

Techniques: Right-angle weave, chainmail variation

Finished size: 22 inches (55.9 cm)

Base

1 Thread the size 10 needle with 4 yards (3.7 m) of conditioned thread. Pick up 12 A beads. Pass through the first nine beads strung to form the first unit, leaving an 18-inch (45.7 cm) tail (figure a). The last three beads will be referred to as the "common wall."

2 Pick up nine A beads. Pass down through the common wall and through the first six beads just strung (figure b).

3 Pick up nine A beads. Pass up through the common wall and through the first six beads just strung (figure c).

4 Repeat steps 2 and 3 to make a right-angle weave chain with a total of 97 units, gradually transitioning from A beads to B beads. Note: Any adjustments in length must be made in increments of seven units. Repeat the last unit's thread path to reinforce; exit from the center bead of the last common wall.

5 Pick up one bead cap from outside to inside, one daisy spacer (if necessary to fill the cap, stabilizing the bead), and the focal bead. If the focal bead's hole is wide, pick up enough size 11° seed beads to fill the hole. Pick up another daisy spacer if necessary, one bead cap from inside to outside, three size 15° seed beads, the drop bead, and three more size 15° seed beads. Pass back through the bead cap and the rest of the beads strung in this step to form a focal dangle. Pass through the center bead of the last common wall from the bead's opposite side so the focal dangle is centered beneath this bead (figure d).

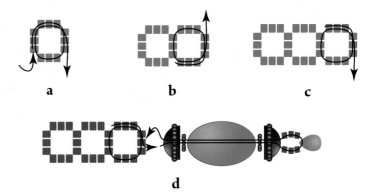

a   b   c

d

copper clusters lariat

6 Weave through the beads of the last unit on the chain and through the focal dangle beads again to reinforce. Repeat once more to strengthen. You may need to switch to the size 12 needle to fit through the beads. Secure the working thread and trim; don't trim the tail thread. Set the beadwork aside.

Cluster 1

7 Condition and prepare the jump rings, opening them a little wider than you would for regular chainmail. Open half of the 5-mm jump rings, close the other half; open all the 5.5-mm jump rings; and open all of the 4-mm jump rings.

8 Place one closed 5-mm jump ring on an open 5-mm jump ring. Use bent chain-nose pliers to hold the 5-mm open jump ring (figure e). Attach the open jump ring to the top of the right-angle weave unit closest to the focal dangle so that the closed jump ring sits on the front of the beadwork. Add another closed 5-mm jump ring to the open jump ring, this time so that it sits on the back of the beadwork (figure f). Close the jump ring around the top side of the unit (figure g).

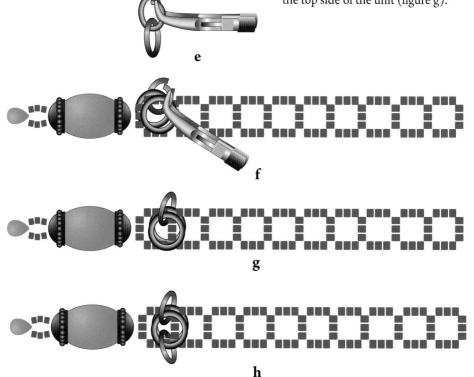

e

f

g

h

9 Use one 5-mm open jump ring to connect both of the closed jump rings placed in step 8 to the bottom of the same unit (figure h).

10 Use one 5.5-mm jump ring to connect both closed jump rings placed in step 8 to the top of the next unit in the chain (figure i).

11 Use one 5.5-mm jump ring to connect both closed jump rings placed in step 8 to the bottom of the next unit in the chain (figure j).

12 Use a 4-mm jump ring to lock the last 5.5-mm jump ring in place (figure k). Insert the 4-mm jump ring through the last 5.5-mm jump ring, then go around the bottom of the next unit. Flip the work over so you can maneuver the 4-mm jump ring around the beads, but keep it inside the 5.5-mm jump ring. This takes a bit of coaxing, but can be done by pushing up the 5.5-mm jump ring with your finger while using pliers to pull the 4-mm jump ring down and outward. This seems to work best if the 4-mm jump ring is opened a bit wider than usual. Close the jump ring (figure l).

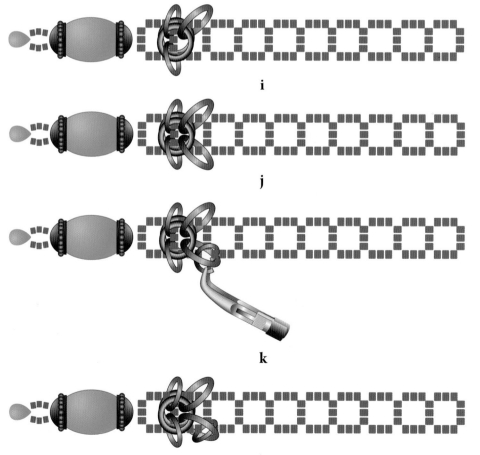

i

j

k

l

copper clusters lariat

13 Repeat step 12 on the other side of the beadwork (figure m).

Cluster 2

14 Begin in the same unit as the 4-mm jump rings from cluster 1 to repeat steps 8 through 13 (figure n).

Cluster 3

15 Begin in the same unit as the 4-mm jump rings from cluster 2 to repeat steps 8 through 13.

16 Skip a unit and repeat clusters 1 through 3 (figure o). Continue in this fashion to the end, but don't attach the 4-mm jump rings on the last cluster.

Finishing

17 Place a size 10 needle on the tail thread. With the thread exiting up through the end common wall, pick up three A beads, skip two jump ring clusters on the chain, and pass down through the common wall between the second and third clusters (figure p). Pick up three A beads. Pass through the end common wall to form the final unit, forming a loop in the chain (figure q). Check that the focal dangle fits through the loop and make any adjustments if necessary. Repeat the thread path of the final unit several times to reinforce. Secure the thread and trim. Attach the final two 4-mm jump rings to complete cluster 3.

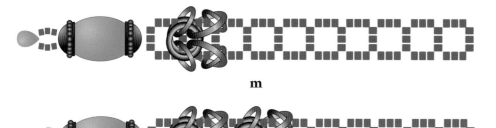

m

n

o

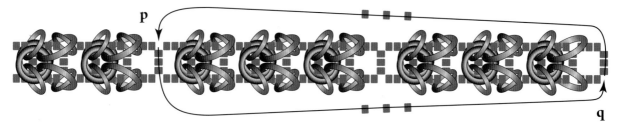

p

q

triad ring

Use flat peyote stitch to form a smooth, comfortable beaded band with "holes" built right in for some beadmaille-style embellishment.

triad ring

Supplies

Fuchsia size D nylon beading thread

Rhubarb luster size 11° cylinder beads, 3 g

8 copper 18-gauge open jump rings, 3 mm I.D.

3 copper 18-gauge open jump rings, 4.5 mm I.D.

Thread conditioner

Size 13 beading needle

Scissors

Thread burner

Bead clamps or stops

Bent chain-nose pliers, 2 pairs

Techniques: Peyote stitch, square stitch, chainmail variation

Finished size: ¼-inch (6 mm) wide

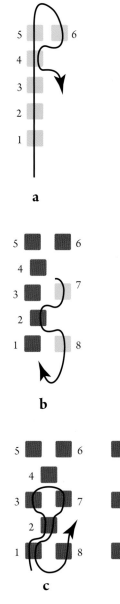

a

b

1. Place a bead clamp 6 inches (15.2 cm) from the end of 5 feet (1.5 m) of conditioned thread. Place the needle on the other end. Pick up six beads. Pass back through the fourth bead strung (figure a).

2. Pick up one bead, skip the next bead strung in step 1, pass through the following bead, and pick up one more bead (figure b).

3. Pass through the first, second, and third beads strung in step 1; the second bead added in step 2 (marked "7" in figure c); back through the second and first beads from step 1; and through the last bead placed (marked "8" in figure c). This figure-eight turnaround positions the needle for the next row and is required for every other row.

4. Pick up one bead, skip one bead, and pass through the next bead; repeat (figure d).

5. Repeat step 3 to work another row of odd-count peyote stitch. Remove the bead clamp.

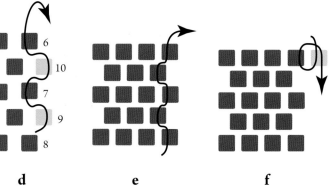

c   **d**   **e**   **f**

6 Repeat steps 4 and 5 once. Repeat step 4 and weave back through the beads to exit from the edge of the first bead added in the row (figure e).

7 Pick up one bead. Pass through the last bead exited and the bead just added to make a square stitch (figure f).

8 Pick up two beads. Stretch the strand across the previous row and square stitch the second bead just added to the adjacent bead on the left (figure g). Repeat this sequence once (figure h).

9 Work a row of peyote stitch, attaching the last bead by starting a figure-eight turnaround as before (figure i), but weave through the beads to exit out from the first bead added in this row (figure j).

10 Repeat steps 7, 8, and 9, reversing directions in each set, until there are eight pairs of holes in the beadwork (figure k).

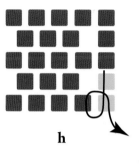

g

h

i

j

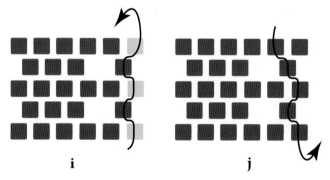

k

triad ring

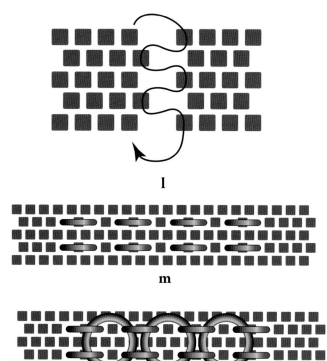

l

m

n

11 Work odd-count peyote stitch until the strip is long enough to wrap comfortably around your finger; end with an even-numbered row. Forty beads along the edge (a total of 80 rows) makes a size 9 ring; 41 beads along the edge (a total of 82 rows) makes a size 10 ring. Adding or subtracting two rows will change the ring about one size.

12 Fold the beadwork so that the first and last rows meet and the beads interlock like a zipper. Taking care that the strip isn't twisted, weave back and forth through the beads to close the beadwork into a tube (figure l). Secure the thread and trim.

13 Attach one 3-mm jump ring horizontally through the first pair of holes in the beadwork; repeat to create two parallel rows of four rings each (figure m).

14 Use the 4.5-mm jump rings to connect the horizontal pairs of 3-mm jump rings to each other (figure n).

variation

foxtail necklace

This arresting necklace uses tubular right-angle weave to create individual chain links with a beaded cage for a luminous resin bead.

foxtail necklace

Supplies

Dark green size D nylon beading thread

Size 11° seed beads:

    Matte green iris, 40 g (A)

    Semi-matte slate blue grey, 10 g (B)

Size 15° seed beads:

    Matte green iris, 5 g (C)

    Semi-matte slate blue grey, 5 g (D)

12 sterling silver decorative round rings, 18 mm O.D.

48 aquamarine bicone crystal beads, 3 mm

1 light blue round resin bead, 20 mm

2 sterling silver 18-gauge open jump rings, 4 mm I.D.

1 sterling silver box clasp, 15 mm

Thread conditioner

Size 12 and 13 beading needles, 2 or more

Scissors

Thread burner

Techniques: Tubular right-angle weave, foxtail chain variation

Finished size: 19 inches (48.3 cm)

Note: Work with a size 12 needle and tight thread tension throughout this project. If necessary, switch to a size 13 needle to pass through beads filled with thread.

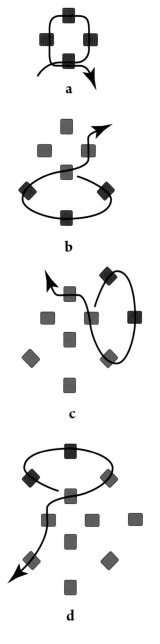

a

b

c

d

Making foxtail links

1   Use 3 yards (2.7 m) of stretched and conditioned thread to pick up AAAA. Pass through the first beads, leaving a 12-inch (30.5 cm) tail (figure a). This will be the bottom, or "floor," of the first three-dimensional unit.

2   Pick up AAA. Pass through the first and second floor beads (figure b).

3   Pick up AA. Pass through the first bead added in the previous unit (the "common wall"), and the second and third floor beads (figure c).

4   Pick up AA. Pass through the common wall of the previous unit, the third and fourth floor beads, and pass up through the nearest common wall of the first unit (figure d).

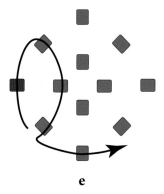

e

5 Pick up A. Pass down through the previous common wall, through the fourth floor bead, up through the first unit's common wall, and through the second bead added in step 2 (figure e).

6 Weave through the four top beads of the units added in steps 2 through 5 and pull tight to create a tiny cube (figure f). The last four beads passed through will be the floor beads for the next cube.

7 Repeat steps 2 through 6, working as in figures g, h, i, and j, to complete a total of five adjoining cubes.

8 Pick up AAA. Pass through the first and second floor beads (figure k).

9 Pick up A. Pass down through the common wall of the previous unit and through the second and third floor beads (figure l).

g

h

i

j

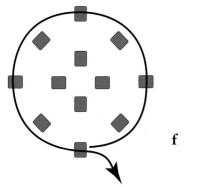

f

k   **l**

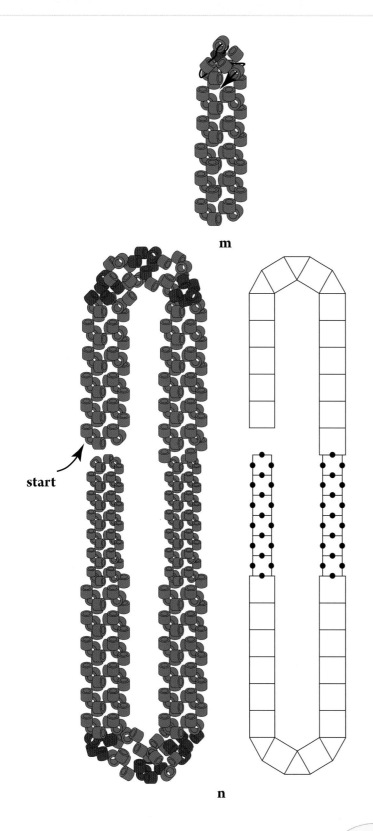

m

start

n

10 Pick up A. Pass through the nearest top bead of the cube added in step 8, the A bead added in step 9, and the third, fourth, and first floor beads to complete a 45° unit (figure m), shown with orange beads in figure n.

11 Weave through the beads to exit up through a common wall on the inside top of the angled cube. Use A beads to work a cube as in steps 2 through 6, shown in green in figure n. Use A beads to work one angled cube as in step 10, one regular cube, and one more angled cube to create a curve in the beadwork.

12 Use A beads to work five regular cubes. Work one cube using A beads for the common walls and C beads for the unit tops. Use C beads to work six cubes (indicated with dots in figure n).

13 Use A beads to work six cubes.

14 Weave through the beads to exit from the top bead on the right side of the final cube. Repeat steps 8 through 12 to form the link's mirrored curve. Use A beads to right-angle weave the top of the final cube to the bottom of the first cube. Secure the thread and trim. Set the foxtail link aside.

15 Repeat steps 1 through 14 to work a total of two A-bead/C-bead foxtail links and four B-bead/D-bead foxtail links.

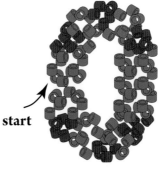

Making basic links

16 Use 1 yard (.9 m) of stretched and conditioned thread and A beads to repeat steps 1 through 6, then repeat steps 8 through 10. Repeat four times to form a total of five regular and five angled cubes that curve into a tubular right-angle weave ring. Repeat steps 1 through 6 (figure o). Insert two decorative rings. Use A beads and the right-angle weave thread path of the angled cube to connect the top of the final cube to the bottom of the first cube. Set the basic link aside.

17 Repeat step 16, but before closing the link, slip on only one decorative ring and one of the decorative rings added to the first link. Continue in this fashion to form a chain with five beaded links connected by six decorative rings. Set the chain aside.

18 Repeat steps 16 and 17 to form another chain.

Making connecting links

19 Use 1 yard (.9 m) of stretched and conditioned thread and A beads to stitch a link like figure p; don't stitch the link closed or trim the thread. Set the link aside. Repeat to form a second A-bead link.

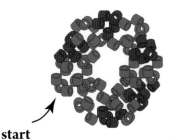

start

o

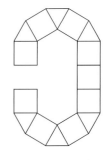

start

p

foxtail necklace

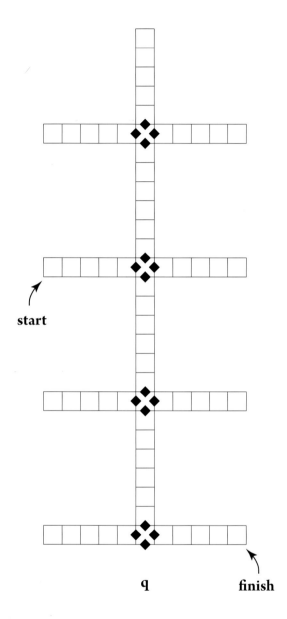

start

q   **finish**

Focal bead

20 Unspool, stretch, and condition 3 yards (2.7 m) of thread; don't cut it from the spool. Place a needle at the end of the thread. Use A beads to work four regular cubes. Work one cube with A beads for the walls and crystals for the unit tops. Work one regular cube with crystal beads. Work five more regular cubes with A beads. Weave through the beads to exit from a crystal bead at the center of the row. Using the top four crystals as the floor beads, use A beads to work five regular cubes upward from the crystal-bead cube. Work one cube with A beads for the walls and crystals for the unit tops. Use crystal beads to work one regular cube. Follow the top half of figure q to work A-bead cube rows and the top half of the center column. Each row and column will be intersected by a crystal-bead cube. Don't trim the thread; leave the needle attached.

21 Unspool and cut 3 yards (2.7 m) of thread. Stretch and condition the thread and place a needle on the end. Weave through the beads to exit from the bottom of the nearest crystal cube. Working downward, follow the bottom half of figure q to work the remaining A-bead rows and the bottom half of the center column, intersected by crystal-bead cubes as before. Don't trim the thread; leave the needle attached.

Assembly

22 Fold the beadwork up so that the crystal-bead cube at the center of the bottom row touches the top A-bead cube of the center column. This is now the top. Place the resin bead inside the fold. Bring all four row ends on the right side together so that they form a cross. Weave the working thread from step 21 through the beads to exit from a top A bead at the end of a row on the right side of the resin bead. Pass through the last A bead of each row end that's touching the resin bead (figure r).

23 While the thread is still loose, slide a B-bead foxtail link around the top row between the beadwork and the resin bead on the left side. The size 15° bead area of the link should be positioned under the top row. Position another B-bead link on the right side.

24 Use the working thread remaining from step 20 to weave through the beadwork to exit from a top A bead in the center column. Use A beads and a right-angle weave thread path to connect the top of the A-bead cube to the bottom of the crystal-bead cube in the center of the bottom row. Secure and trim this thread only.

25 Use the working thread to repeat the step 22 thread path two times, tightening the now floor beads. Weave through the beads to exit through what is now a top bead. Pick up AAA. Pass through the last top bead exited (figure s).

26 Pass through the first two A beads just strung. Pick up one A bead, pass through the top bead at the edge of the opposite row end, pick up another A bead, and pass through the second and third beads added in step 25 (figure t).

27 Weave through the beadwork following the path in figure u twice to secure the connection.

28 Weave through the beadwork to close the row ends on the left side of the bead in the same fashion as in steps 22 through 27. Secure the thread and trim.

29 Slide an A-bead foxtail link through both ends of one of the B-bead foxtail links attached to the focal. Pinch the ends together. Slide a B-bead foxtail link through the A-bead foxtail link. Pinch the ends together.

30 Use one connector link to connect both ends of the B-bead foxtail link and the last decorative ring of one of the chains. Use A beads and a right-angle weave thread path to stitch the connection link closed.

31 Repeat steps 29 and 30 to assemble the other chain.

32 Use one jump ring to attach the open link at each chain end to one half of the clasp.

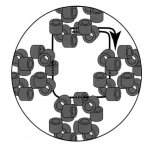

r

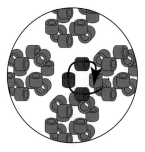

s

t

u

faerie garden necklace

Weave ring triads into formation with seed beads
and make a lacy edge to this pretty necklace.

Supplies

Smoke 6-pound (2.7 k) braided
    beading thread

Size 11° seed beads:

Pink-lined olivine,
    5 g (A)

Matte transparent raspberry,
    2 g (B)

36 silver decorative rings,
    9 mm O.D.

1 sterling silver hook-and-eye
    clasp, 40 mm

Thread conditioner

Size 12 beading needle

Scissors

Thread burner

Techniques: Right-angle
    weave, European chainmail
    variation

Finished size: 18 inches
    (45.7 cm)

Focal

1 Unspool and condition 3 yards
(2.7 m) of thread; don't trim
it from the spool. Pick up AA,
ABA, AA, ABA, and one ring;
pass through all the beads again
to form the first right-angle weave
unit that captures the ring. Pass
through the first seven beads
strung to exit down through the
ring (figure a). The last two beads
exited will be referred to as the
"common wall." Note: Keep tight
thread tension and be sure the
rings are popped down as you
work this project.

2 Pick up ABA, AA, and ABA. Pass
down through the common wall
to place one unit on each side of
the ring (figure b).

3 Pick up AAABAAA, AA, AAA-
BAAA, and one ring. Pass down
through the common wall, capturing the ring you just exited. This
will form a long unit which will
become one leg of a triangle. Pass
through the first five beads of the
unit added in step 2 (figure c).

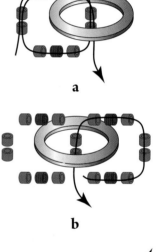

a

b

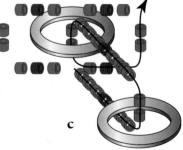

c

faerie garden necklace

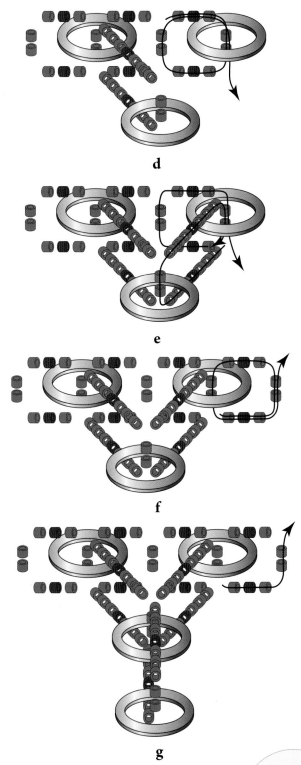

d

e

f

g

4 Pick up ABA, AA, ABA, and one ring. Pass up through the common wall and the first five beads just strung, capturing the new ring (figure d).

5 Pick up AAABAAA to make the bottom of a new long unit. Pass up through the common wall at the end of the first long unit from step 3. Pick up AAABAAA to make the top of the new long unit. Pass down through the common wall, then through all the beads of the unit formed in step 4, exiting down through the ring (figure e).

6 Pick up ABA, AA, and ABA. Pass down through the common wall, capturing the ring. Pass through the first five beads just strung to exit the top side of the common wall (figure f). This completes one triangle.

7 Repeat step 4, then steps 2 through 6 to make a second triangle.

8 Repeat step 7 to form two more triangles for a total of four triangles. Weave through the beads to exit from the common wall at the tip of the fourth triangle. Add one long unit by picking up AAABAAA, AA, AAABAAA, and one ring. Pass through the common wall. Weave through the beads to exit from the top of the last common wall formed in step 7 (figure g).

9 Repeat step 7 to form three more triangles for a total of seven triangles.

Sides

10 Pick up ABA, A, and ABA. Pass up through the common wall and the first four beads just strung to exit from the bottom of the common wall (figure h). The common wall is now just one bead.

11 Pick up ABA, A, ABA, and one ring. Pass through the common wall and the first four beads just strung, capturing the ring.

12 Pick up ABA, A, and ABA. Pass through the common wall and the first four beads just strung, capturing the ring.

13 Pick up ABA, A, and ABA. Pass through the common wall and the first four beads just strung.

14 Repeat steps 11 through 13 six more times to add a total of seven rings.

15 Pick up AAA, one clasp half, and AAA. Pass through the common wall (figure i). Retrace the thread path of the final unit several times to reinforce. Secure the working thread and trim.

16 Unspool 1 yard (.9 m) of thread at the other end of the focal. Cut, condition, and add a needle to the thread. Repeat steps 10 through 15 to mirror the first side of the necklace.

variation

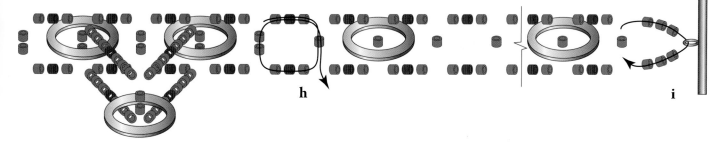

h

i

This trio of textured beaded circles connected with chain and links makes a pretty and versatile necklace appropriate for any occasion.

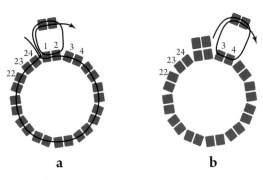

Supplies

Smoke 8-pound (3.6 k) braided beading thread

Matte dark copper size 11° seed beads, 5 g (A)

Matte metallic khaki 3.4 mm pressed-glass drop beads, 7 g

Bronze copper size 15° seed beads, 2 g (B)

Antiqued brass 3-mm rolo/12-mm flat oval combination chain, 2 feet (61 cm)

7 antiqued brass 18-gauge open jump rings, 8 mm O.D.

4 antiqued brass 21-gauge open jump rings, 4 mm O.D.

Antiqued brass 24-gauge round wire, 10 inches (25.4 cm)

4 antiqued brass daisy spacers, 5 mm

15 assorted olive and topaz pressed-glass beads, 3 to 4 mm

1 antiqued brass lobster claw clasp, 10 mm

2 brass hourglass tube beads, 4 x 8 mm

Thread conditioner

Size 12 beading needle

Scissors

Thread burner

Flush cutters

Various pliers

Techniques: Square stitch, wrapped loop

Finished size: 23 inches (58.4 cm)

Rounds 1 and 2

1 Use 2 yards (1.8 m) of conditioned thread to pick up 24 A beads, leaving a 1 yard (.9 m) tail. Tie a knot with the working and tail threads to form a snug base circle. Pass through the first two beads strung.

2 Pick up AA, pass through the first two base circle beads and the two beads just strung to form a square stitch (figure a).

3 Pick up AA. Pass through the next two beads of the first round, and the two beads just strung (figure b).

4 Using tight tension, repeat step 3 around the circle to add a round of square stitch. Pass through the first two beads of the second round to tighten the beadwork.

a   **b**

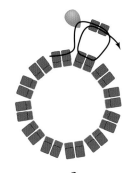

c

d

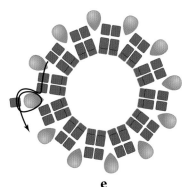

e

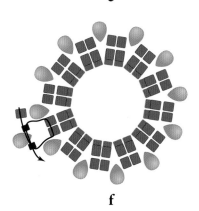

f

Round 3

5 Pick up one drop bead and AA. Pass through the first pair of A beads added in round 2, skip the drop bead, and pass through the two A beads just strung (figure c). Repeat around the circle. Exit from two A beads.

Round 4

6 Move the needle to the tail and flip the work over. Work in the opposite direction to form a round parallel to Round 3. Pick up one drop bead and AA. Pass through the last pair of A beads added in Round 1, skip the drop bead, and pass through the two A beads just strung (figure d). Repeat around the circle. Exit from two A beads.

Round 5

7 Pick up one A bead. Pass through the nearest drop bead and through the A bead just strung (figure e).

8 Pick up B, one drop bead, and B. Pass through the next pair of A beads from round 4 and the B/drop bead/B sequence to tighten (figure f).

9 Repeat steps 7 and 8 around the circle. Attach round 5 to round 3 by stitching B/one drop bead/B from round 5 to pairs of A beads from round 3. Secure the thread and trim. Set the ring aside.

10 Repeat steps 1 through 9 to form two more beaded rings.

Assembly

11 Cut the chain into one ¾-inch (1.9 cm) and two 9½-inch (24.1 cm) pieces. Set the pieces aside.

12 Gently insert one 8-mm jump ring to connect one 9½-inch (24.1 cm) chain to a beaded ring at the twelve-o'clock position, passing through the ring's rounds 3, 4, and 5; close the ring (figure g). Use one 8-mm jump ring to connect one end of a ring link to the same beaded ring at the six-o'clock position (figure h). Set the beaded ring aside. Repeat this step for the second beaded ring.

13 Use one 8-mm jump ring to connect the open end of the first beaded ring's link (placed in step 12) to the third beaded ring at the two-o'clock position (figure i). Repeat to connect the open end of the second beaded ring's link to the third beaded ring at the ten-o'clock position. Use one 8-mm jump ring to connect the remaining ring link to the third beaded ring at the six-o'clock position (figure j).

14 Use one 4-mm jump ring to connect the bottom ring link to the ¾-inch (2.5 cm) length of chain (figure k).

15 Cut 2 inches (5.1 cm) of wire. Form a wrapped loop at one end, but before making the wrap slip on a drop bead. Trim the wrap. Use the wire to string on an assortment of three pressed-glass beads. Form another wrapped loop that attaches to the open end link of the ¾-inch (1.9 cm) chain. Repeat four times to make a total of five assorted dangles. Use the 4-mm jump rings to evenly space the dangles up the length of the chain (figure l).

16 Use the remaining 4-mm jump rings to attach the clasp to the chain ends.

g

h

i

j

k

l

london flat bracelet

Softly draping, fluid, intriguing . . . just a few words that describe this bracelet. Create it by surrounding hammered rings with a cage of three-dimensional right-angle weave.

Supplies

Peach size D nylon beading thread

Size 11° seed beads:

    Silver-lined salmon alabaster, 8 g (A)

    Silver-lined matte brown AB, 2 g (B)

21 gold oval hammered rings, 13 x 18 mm O.D.

1 gold 20 mm toggle bar, 20 mm

Thread conditioner

Size 10 beading needle

Scissors

Thread burner

Techniques: Right-angle weave, European chainmail variation

Finished size: 7¾ inches (19.7 cm)

1   Thread the needle with 4 yards (3.7 m) of conditioned thread. Pick up 14 beads in this order: ABA, AAAA, ABA, and AAAA. Pick up one ring, leaving a 12-inch (30.5-cm) tail. Pass through the first 10 beads and the ring to form the first right-angle weave unit (figure a). The last three beads exited will be referred to as the "common wall." The thread should exit the bottom of the common wall, below the ring.

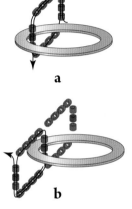

a

b

2   Pick up AAAA, ABA, and AAAA. Pass down through the common wall and continue through the first seven beads just added to exit up from the second unit's common wall (figure b). The two units will sit on either side of the ring.

3   Pick up AABAA, ABA, and AABAA. Pass up through the last common wall exited and continue through the first eight beads just added (figure c).

c

4   Pick up AAAA, ABA, and AAAA. Pass up through the first ring added and pick up one new ring. Pass down through the last common wall exited and continue through the first seven beads just added, capturing both rings (figure d).

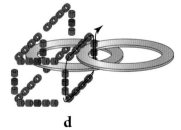

d

london flat bracelet

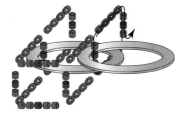

e

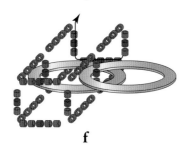

f

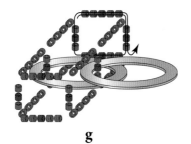

g

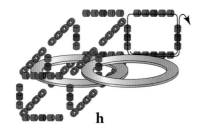

h

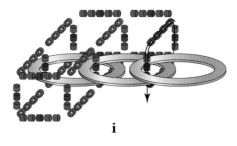

i

5 Pick up AAAA, ABA, and AAAA. Pass up through the last common wall exited and continue through the first seven beads just added (figure e).

6 Pick up AABAA. Pass up through the common wall of the first unit (figure f). Pick up AABAA. Pass down through the previous common wall to finish the unit. Pass through the entire unit again to reinforce, exiting down through the previous common wall (figure g).

7 Pick up AABAA, ABA, and AABAA. Pass down through the last common wall exited and continue through the first eight beads just strung (figure h).

8 Pick up AAAA, ABA, AAAA, and one ring. Pass down through the last ring placed, up through the last common wall exited, and continue through the first seven beads just added (figure i).

9 Pick up AAAA, ABA, and AAAA. Pass down through the last common wall exited and continue through the first seven beads just added (figure j).

10 Pick up AABAA. Pass down through the adjacent common wall on this side of the chain (figure k). Pick up AABAA and pass up through the previous common wall to finish the unit. Pass through the entire unit to reinforce (figure l).

11 Repeat steps 3 through 10 to add a total of 21 rings. The final ring will serve as the clasp ring.

12 Weave through the beads in the final units to reinforce the clasp ring connection. Secure the working thread and trim.

13 Weave the tail thread through the beads to exit up from the common wall between the first two units. Pick up AAAAAA, the toggle bar, and AAAAAA. Pass up through the same common wall to form a loop (figure m). Weave through the beads in the final units to reinforce the toggle bar connection. Secure the tail thread and trim.

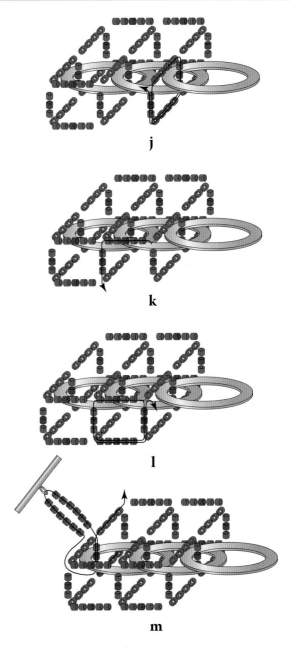

j

k

l

m

variation

spiral chain necklace

A twisting chain dotted with luminous drop beads makes a versatile necklace.

Supplies

Smoke 6-pound (2.7 k) braided beading thread

1 sterling silver toggle clasp, 14 mm

Size 11° seed beads:

Matte metallic midnight blue iris, 5 g (A)

Gold-lined ice blue, 5 g (B)

50 black AB Czech glass drop beads, 4 x 6 mm

1 sterling silver wire protector, 4.6 x 4mm (.56 mm I.D.)

150 sterling silver 18-gauge open jump rings, 4.5 mm I.D.

Thread conditioner

Size 10 beading needle

Scissors

Thread burner

Various pliers

Techniques: Right-angle weave, spiral chainmail variation

Finished size: 18 inches (45.7 cm)

Note: The necklace shortens when the jump rings are added, so to make a longer necklace, stitch the base beadwork at least 1½ inches (3.7 cm) longer than the desired length.

1 Thread a needle on 4 yards (3.7 m) of conditioned thread. Pick up the toggle ring, AAAAAA, one drop bead, and BBBBBB, leaving a 12-inch (30.5 cm) tail. Pass through all again to form the first right-angle weave unit. Pass through the first six seed beads and the drop bead just strung (figure a).

2 Pick up BBBBBB, one drop bead, and AAAAAA. Pass through the previous drop bead and the six B beads and drop bead just strung to form another unit (figure b).

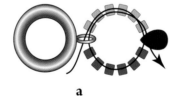

a

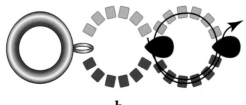

b

spiral chain necklace

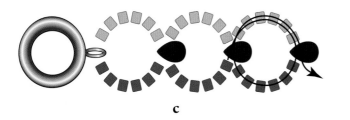

c

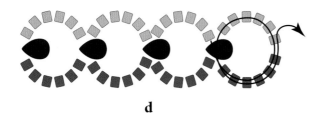

d

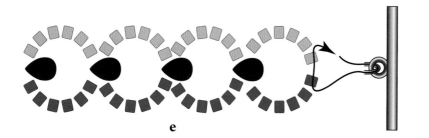

e

3   Pick up AAAAAA, one drop bead, and BBBBBB. Pass through the previous drop bead and the six A beads and drop bead just strung to form another unit (figure c).

4   Repeat steps 2 and 3 for a total of 50 drop beads.

5   Pick up AAAAAA and BBBBBB. Pass through the drop bead of the last unit and the first seven beads just strung (figure d). Pass through one side of the wire protector, pick up the toggle bar, and pass through the other side of the wire protector. Pass through the two end beads on the chain and the wire protector (figure e) several times to reinforce.

6   Repeat the thread path of the entire necklace to reinforce. Secure the thread and trim. Move the needle to the tail thread and weave through the first unit several times to reinforce. Secure the tail thread and trim.

7   Orient the necklace so that the drop beads point upward and the toggle ring is at the bottom.

8 Open all the jump rings. Attach one jump ring through neighboring units so that the jump rings sit on the left side of each drop bead (figure f).

9 Working from the toggle ring up, connect jump rings to the right side of the chain that cross through the original jump rings on the left. To make a smooth connection, scoop down through the bottom of the first existing jump ring through the first beaded unit. Pass under the beads and come up through the next unit on the right side of the drop bead. Close the jump ring (figure g). Repeat to the end, making sure all the drop beads point upwards.

10 Working from the toggle ring up, add a third row of jump rings to connect the previous two rows. Make the connections by scooping behind and up through the top of the right jump ring of the first pair, staying on the top of the beads. Continue to scoop around the left edge on the outside of the beaded unit and come up through the second unit from the back. Pass through the back of the left jump ring from the next pair (figure h). Repeat to the end to create a gentle twist in the chain.

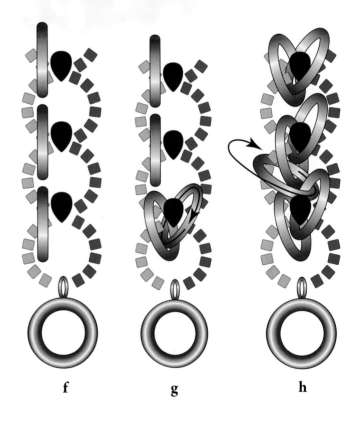

f   g   h

two-tone doublewide cuff

The chainmail in this substantial cuff stands out with strips of contrasting beadwork. The color and placement of the jump rings emphasize the two-tone metallic asterisk pattern.

Supplies

Smoke 10-pound braided beading thread

Dark blue luster size 11° cylinder beads, 5 g

186 silver 18-gauge open jump rings, 3.5 mm I.D.

314 brass 18-gauge open jump rings, 3.5 mm I.D.

1 sterling silver toggle clasp, 10 mm

Thread conditioner

Size 10 beading needle

Scissors

Thread burner

Various pliers

Techniques: Right-angle weave, Japanese 12-2 chainmail variation

Finished size: 7¼ inches (18.4cm)

1 Thread the needle with 1 yard (.9 m) of conditioned thread. Pick up 14 beads, leaving a 6-inch (15.2 cm) tail. Pass through all the beads again to form a right-angle weave unit. Pass through the first eight beads just strung (figure a). The last bead exited will be referred to as the "connecting bead."

a

2 Pick up 13 beads. Pass though the connecting bead from the previous unit and the first seven beads just added (figure b). Keep a moderate thread tension as you work; if your tension is too tight, the jump rings added in steps 5 through 8 won't fit.

b

3 Repeat step 2 to form a total of 18 units, or long enough to reach your desired length minus 1½ inches (3.8 cm). Don't knot or trim the working thread. Secure the tail thread and trim; set the beaded strip aside.

4 Repeat steps 1 through 3 to form two more strips.

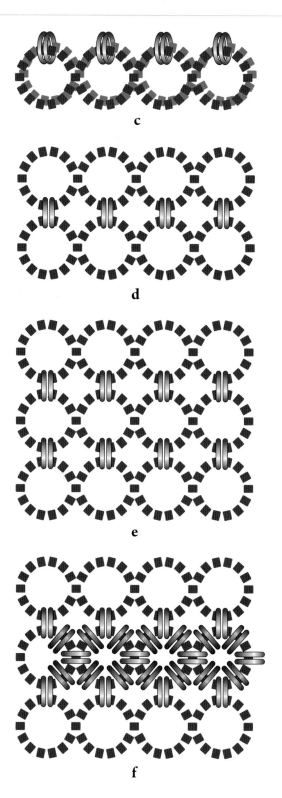

c

d

e

f

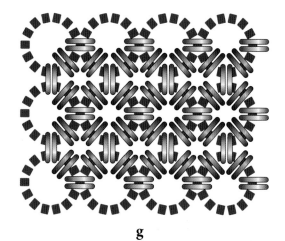

g

5 Lay two beaded strips on top of each other. Use two silver jump rings to connect each set of beaded circles along one edge of strips (figure c). Separate the strips so that the beadwork is single layered with the jump rings down the center (figure d).

6 Stack the third strip on top of the second strip and use two silver jump rings to connect each set of beaded circles along the open edge. Separate the strips as before (figure e).

7 Use two silver jump rings to connect each set of beaded circles within the second strip; the jump rings will encircle this strip's connecting beads. Attach two brass jump rings to the second strip between each set of silver jump rings, creating an asterisk pattern. All vertical and horizontal jump rings should be silver, all diagonal jump rings brass (figure f).

8 Repeat step 7, this time making half an asterisk pattern down the first and third strips (figure g).

9 Connect two brass jump rings to the end of the first strip; four brass jump rings to the end of the second strip; and two brass jump rings to the end of the third strip (figure h). Separate the four brass jump rings at the end of the second strip into two pairs. Use two silver jump rings to connect the jump ring pair at the end of the first strip to the closest pair at the end of the second strip; repeat to connect the jump rings at the end of the second and third strips (figure i). Connect one brass jump ring to each set of silver rings just placed (figure j); attach the clasp ring to these two brass jump rings (figure k).

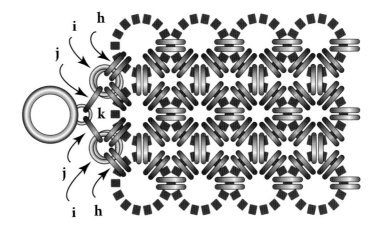

10 Check the bracelet for fit and make adjustments as necessary. Secure all thread and trim. Repeat step 9 to add the clasp bar to the other end of the bracelet.

seashell pendant

Create a sculpted pendant with different colors inside and out, just like its natural inspiration.

Supplies

Cream size D nylon beading thread

Size 11° seed beads:

Transparent golden berry shimmer, 8 g (A)

Dusty mauve-lined amber, 2 g (B)

Gold-lined cream, 8 g (C)

2 silver decorative round rings, 9 mm O.D.

1 silver decorative round ring, 13 mm O.D.

1 silver decorative round ring, 18 mm O.D.

2 silver decorative oval rings, 8 x 13 mm O.D.

2 silver decorative oval rings, 13 x 18 mm O.D.

Sterling silver 21-gauge round half-hard wire, 3 inches (7.6 cm)

1 dark topaz fire-polished round bead, 8 mm

2 pink opal rondelle beads, 10 x 8 mm

Thread conditioner

Size 12 and 13 beading needles

Scissors

Thread burner

Various pliers

Flush cutters

Techniques: Right-angle weave, European chainmail variation

Finished size: 2⅜ x 1½ inches (6 x 3.8 cm)

Note: The pendant's construction is based on the London Flat Bracelet (page 88), so it would be helpful to familiarize yourself with its technique and instructions first.

Making the base

1 Unspool and condition 3 yards (2.7 m) of thread; don't cut the thread from the spool. Pick up BB, AAA, BB, and CCC. Pass through the first nine beads to form the first right-angle weave unit. The last two beads exited will be referred to as the "common wall."

2 Pick up CCC, BB, and AAA. Pass down through the common wall and through the first five beads just strung to exit up from the second unit's common wall.

3 Pick up AAA, BB, and CCC. Pass up through the common wall and through the first five beads just strung.

4 Pick up CCC, BB, AAA, and one 9-mm ring. Pass down through the common wall, capturing the ring. Pass through the first five beads just added.

5 Pick up AAA. Pass down through the common wall between the first and second units. Pick up CCC. Pass up through the common wall of the last unit.

6 Pick up AAA, BB, and CCC. Pass up through the last common wall exited and through the first five beads just added.

7 Pick up CCC. Pass up through the common wall of the first unit. Pick up AAA. Pass down through the last common wall exited to finish the unit (figure a).

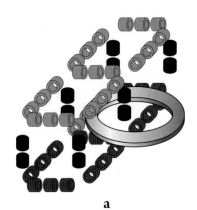

a

seashell pendant

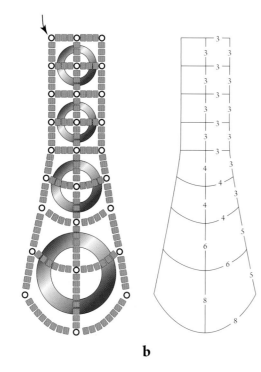

b

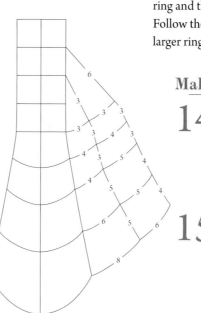

c

8 Pick up CCC, BB, and AAA. Pass down through the common wall and through the first five beads just strung.

9 Pick up AAA, BB, and CCC. Pass up through the common wall and through the five beads just strung.

10 Pick up CCC. Pass up through the common wall between the previous two parallel units, capturing the ring. Pick up AAA. Pass down through the common wall of the last unit.

11 Pick up CCC, BB, and AAA. Pass down through the last common wall exited and through the first five beads just strung.

12 Pick up AAA. Pass down through the adjacent common wall on this side of the chain. Pick up CCC and pass up through the previous common wall to finish the unit.

13 Repeat steps 3 through 12 to add subsequent rings as in figure b, except work the next units around a 13-mm round ring and the following units around an 18-mm round ring. Follow the bead counts on figure b, to accommodate for the larger ring sizes.

Making the sides

14 Follow the bead counts in figure c to work two rows of units to one side of the base. Use an 8 x 13-mm oval ring toward the top of the beadwork and a 13 x 18-mm oval ring toward the bottom. Secure the working thread and trim.

15 Unspool 1 yard (.9 m) of thread. Cut and condition the thread and place a needle at the end. Repeat step 14 to form the other side of the pendant. Secure the thread and trim.

Assembly

16 Form a simple loop at the end of the 21-gauge wire. String on one rondelle. Pinch up the sides of the pendant and pass the wire through the bottom of the outermost angled unit at the top of the pendant. String on one 8-mm bead and pass the wire down through the top of the corresponding unit on the other side of the pendant. String on one rondelle (figure d). Snug the beads so that the 8-mm bead sits on top of the second 9-mm ring with both sides of the pendant flaring up and out. Form another simple loop to secure the beads, tightening the beadwork into place.

17 Attach each simple loop to a length of chain and beads to create a necklace.

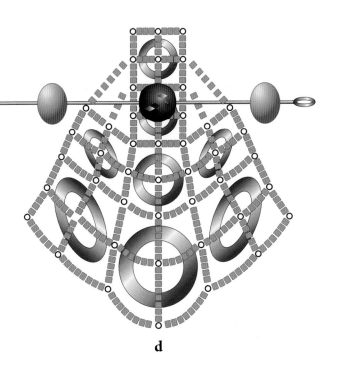

d

x factor bracelet

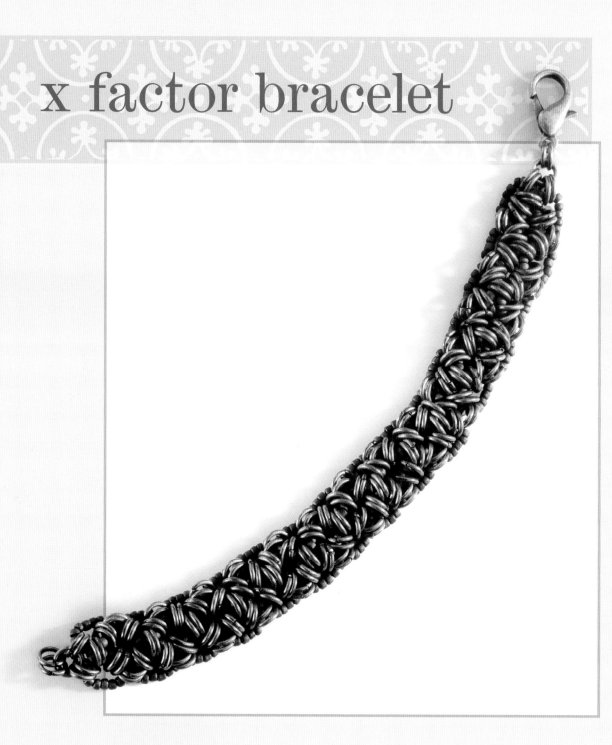

Here's a chunky, funky chainmail bracelet made even more interesting by textured circles of seed beads.

Supplies

Smoke 6-pound (2.7 kg) braided beading thread

Matte metallic moss iris size 11° Japanese seed beads, 6 g

214+ antiqued brass 18-gauge open jump rings, 4 mm I.D.

1 antiqued brass lobster clasp, 12 mm

Thread conditioner

Size 10 beading needle

Scissors

Thread burner

Various pliers

Techniques: Right-angle weave, Japanese 12-2 chainmail variation

Finished size: 7 inches (17.8 cm)

1 Thread the needle with 1 yard (1.8 m) of conditioned thread. Pick up 14 beads. Pass through all the beads again to form the first right-angle weave unit, leaving a 6-inch (15.2 cm) tail. Pass through the first eight beads strung (figure a). The last bead exited will be referred to as the "connecting bead."

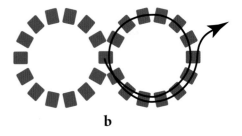

a

2 Pick up 13 beads. Pass through the connecting bead and the first seven beads just strung (figure b).

b

3 Repeat step 2 to form a strip 15 units long or to 1 inch (2.5 cm) less than the desired length. Don't cut the working thread. Move the needle to the tail thread. Secure the tail thread and trim. Set the strip aside.

4 Repeat steps 1 through 3 to form a second strip.

x factor bracelet

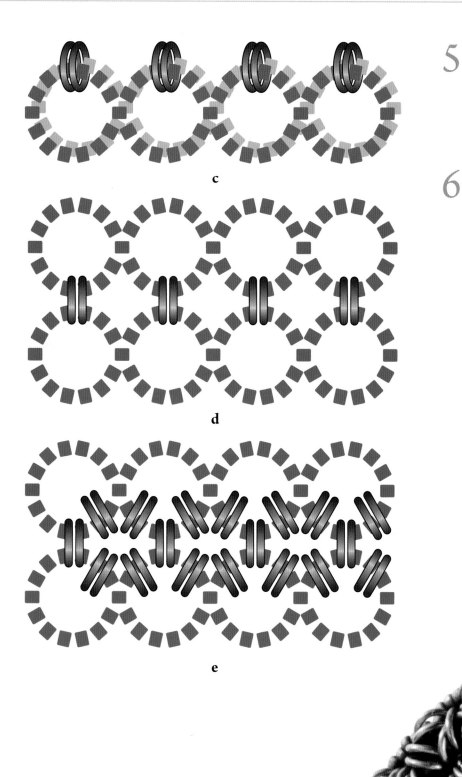

c

d

e

5   Stack the strips so that the units match and the working threads are at the same end. Use pairs of jump rings to connect the units along the top of the strips (figure c). Open the strips so that they lay out flat (figure d).

6   Connect two pairs of jump rings to the lower part of each beaded unit in the top strip so that the pairs sit on each side of the jump rings placed in step 5. Connect two pairs of jump rings to the upper part of each beaded unit in the bottom strip so that the pairs sit on each side of the jump rings placed in step 5. The resulting pattern will make an X shape across the center of the beadwork (figure e).

7 Use pairs of jump rings to connect each adjacent beaded unit around each connecting bead along the top and bottom strips (figure f).

8 Connect one pair of jump rings to each beaded unit at the non-working thread end of the bracelet (figure g). Use two jump rings to connect the last four jump rings placed (figure h).

9 Use one jump ring to connect the clasp to the last two jump rings placed (figure i).

10 Check the bracelet for fit. Make any adjustments to the beading at the other end of the bracelet; secure the thread and trim. Add or remove jump rings as necessary following steps 6 and 7. Repeat step 8.

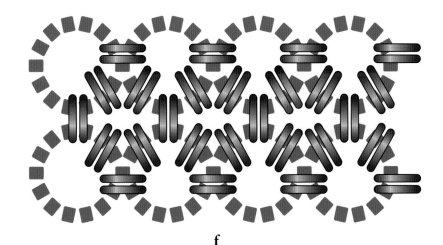

f

h

g

i

g

zinnia necklace

Right-angle weave wedges lock large and small rings into a floral formation. A lovely complement to any outfit.

Supplies

Burgundy size D nylon beading thread

Size 11° seed beads:

Gold-lined cranberry, 2 g (A)

Silver-lined dark coral, 2 g (B)

Silver-lined salmon alabaster, 2 g (C)

Gold-lined peach opal, 2 g (D)

Sterling silver-plated, 2 g (E)

10 silver decorative rings, 9 mm O.D.

3 silver decorative rings, 18 mm O.D.

Sterling silver 8-mm link chain, 4½ feet (1.4 m)

11 sterling silver 20-gauge open jump rings, 4 mm I.D.

1 sterling silver three-loop sliding bar clasp, 20 mm

Thread conditioner

Size 12 and 13 beading needles

Scissors

Thread burner

Wire cutters

Various pliers

Techniques: Right-angle weave, European chainmail variation

Finished size: 18 inches (45.7 cm)

Focal

1 Place the size 12 needle on the end of 2 yards (1.8 m) of conditioned thread. Pick up A, AEA, A, AEA, and one 9-mm ring, leaving a 6-inch (15.2 cm) tail. Pass through the seed beads again to form the first right-angle weave unit. Pass through the first five beads strung to exit below the ring (figure a). The last bead exited will be referred to as the "common wall."

2 Pick up AEA, A, and AEA. Working with tight tension, pass down through the common wall so that the beads capture the ring around the common wall (figure b). Pass through the first four beads just strung to exit up from the common wall. Note: Make sure that as you tighten each unit, the rings are all locked in place on the same side of the beadwork.

3 Pick up AEA, A, AEA, and one 9-mm ring. Pass up through the common wall (figure c) and the first four beads just strung to capture the new ring.

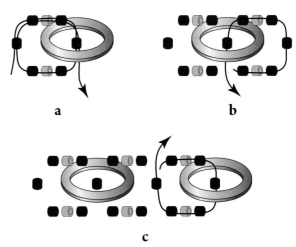

a

b

c

zinnia necklace

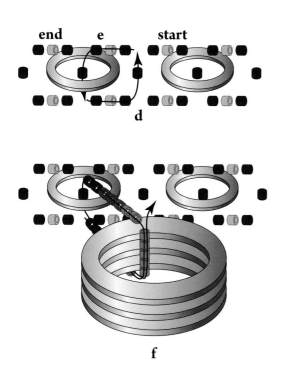

d

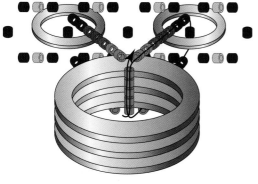

f

g

4 Repeat steps 2 and 3 to create a 10-ring chain. Form a unit by picking up AEA and passing up through the first common wall. Make sure all the 9-mm rings sit on the inside of the ring (figure d). Pick up AEA and pass down through the final common wall, capturing the ring (figure e).

5 Weave through the last unit to reinforce, exiting toward the center of the circle from a bead inside the 9-mm ring.

6 Pick up AABBCDD, DDDDD, DDCBBAA, and three 18-mm rings. Pass down through the common wall, capturing all three rings just strung to form a long unit that will become one leg of a triangle. Pass through the first 12 beads just strung to exit up through the 18-mm rings (figure f).

7 Form the second leg of the triangle by picking up DDCB-BAA. Pass down through the common wall inside the next 9-mm ring of the circle. Pick up AABBCDD and pass up through the common wall at the center of the 18-mm rings (figure g). Pass through the first seven beads strung in this step. Weave through the beads to exit through the common wall inside the following 9-mm ring. One triangle is now complete.

8 Pick up AABBCDD, DDDDD, and DDCBBAA. Pass down through the common wall, capturing the 18-mm rings placed in step 6, and through the first 12 beads just strung to exit up through the 18-mm rings.

9 Form the second leg of the triangle by picking up DDCB-BAA. Pass down through the common wall inside the next 9-mm ring of the circle. Pick up AABBCDD and pass up through the common wall at the center of the 18-mm rings. Pass through the first seven beads strung in this step. Weave through the beads to exit from the common wall inside the following 9-mm ring of the circle. The second triangle is now complete.

10 Repeat steps 8 and 9 for a total of five triangles. Switch to a size 13 needle and repeat the thread path through all the beadwork, especially the triangles, until the beads are full of thread. This will give the pendant more body. Secure the thread and trim.

11 Cut one 16-inch (40.6 cm) piece of chain. Fold the chain in half and use a jump ring to connect the link at the fold to the beadwork between two 9-mm rings, inside one of the triangles (figure h). Cut two 8-inch (20.3 cm) pieces of chain. Use a jump ring to connect one end of one chain to the beadwork so that it sits between the next two 9-mm rings, flanked by two triangles; repeat on the other side of the 16-inch (40.6 cm) chain already placed (figure i). Cut two 8¼-inch (30 cm) pieces of chain. Use a jump ring to connect one end of one chain to the beadwork between two 9-mm rings, inside the next triangle; repeat on the other side of the flower (figure j). Use the remaining jump rings to attach the open chain ends to the clasp.

variation

zinnia bracelet

Show off your beadmaille skills with this pretty flower bracelet. The focal piece stays snugly on top of your wrist with the dangling lampworked beads acting as counterbalances.

Supplies

3 sterling silver headpins, 2 inches (5.1 cm)

4 sterling silver daisy spacers, 4 mm

6 sterling silver bead caps, 6 mm

3 peach/cream/brick lampworked rondelle beads, 12 x 9 mm

Burgundy size D nylon beading thread

Size 11° seed beads:

Gold-lined cranberry, 2 g (A)

Silver-lined dark coral, 2 g (B)

Silver-lined salmon alabaster, 2 g (C)

Gold-lined peach opal, 2 g (D)

Sterling silver-plated, 2 g (E)

10 silver decorative rings, 9 mm O.D.

3 silver decorative rings, 18 mm O.D.

Sterling silver-plated size 15° seed beads, 1 g

12 sterling silver 20-gauge open jump rings, 4 mm I.D.

Sterling silver 8-mm link chain, 18 inches (45.7 cm)

Sterling silver three-loop sliding bar clasp, 20 mm

Thread conditioner

Size 12 and 13 beading needles

Scissors

Thread burner

Wire cutters

Various pliers

Techniques: Right-angle weave, European chainmail variation

Finished size: 6¾ inches (17.1 cm)
The bracelet should be worn snug.

Making the dangles

1   On a headpin, pick up one daisy spacer, one bead cap from outside to inside, one lampworked bead, one bead cap from inside to outside, and one daisy spacer. Form a wrapped loop to secure the beads (figure a). Set the beaded headpin aside. Repeat to make a total of three dangles.

Making the flower

2   Place the size 12 needle on the end of 2 yards (1.8 m) of conditioned thread. Pick up A, AEA, A, AEA, and one 9-mm ring, leaving a 6-inch (15.2 cm) tail. Pass through the seed beads again to form the first right-angle weave unit. Pass through the first five beads strung to exit below the ring (figure b). The last bead exited will be referred to as the "common wall."

3   Pick up AEA, A, and AEA. Working with tight tension, pass down through the common wall so that the beads capture the ring around the common wall (figure c). Pass through the first four beads just strung to exit up from the common wall. Note: Make sure that as you tighten each unit, the rings are all locked in place on the same side of the beadwork.

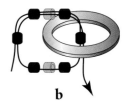

a

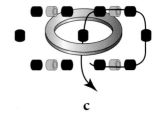

b

c

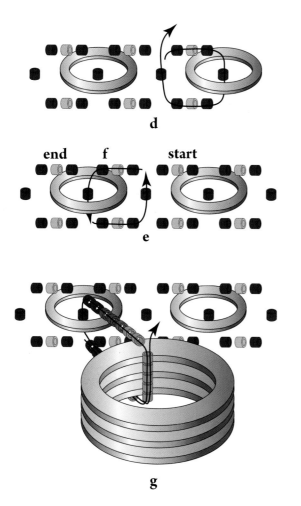

d

end   **f**   **start**

e

g

h

4. Pick up AEA, A, AEA, and one 9-mm ring. Pass up through the common wall (figure d) and the first four beads just strung to capture the new ring.

5. Repeat steps 3 and 4 to create a ten-ring chain. Form a unit by picking up AEA and passing up through the first common wall. Make sure all the 9-mm rings sit on the inside of the ring (figure e). Pick up AEA and pass down through the final common wall, capturing the ring (figure f).

6. Weave through the last unit to reinforce, exiting toward the center of the circle from a bead inside the 9-mm ring.

7. Pick up AABBCDD, DDDDD, DDCBBAA, and three 18-mm rings. Pass down through the common wall, capturing all three rings just strung to form a long unit that will become one leg of a triangle. Pass through the first 12 beads just strung to exit up through the 18-mm rings (figure g).

8. Form the second leg of the triangle by picking up DDCBBAA. Pass down through the common wall inside the next 9-mm ring of the circle. Pick up AABBCDD and pass up through the common wall at the center of the 18-mm rings (figure h). Pass through the first seven beads strung in this step. Weave through the beads to exit through the common wall inside the following 9-mm ring. One triangle is now complete.

9   Pick up AABBCDD, DDDDD, and DDCBBAA. Pass down through the common wall, capturing the 18-mm rings placed in step 7, and through the first 12 beads just strung to exit up through the 18-mm rings.

10 Form the second leg of the triangle by picking up DDCBBAA. Pass down through the common wall inside the next 9-mm ring of the circle. Pick up AABBCDD and pass up through the common wall at the center of the 18-mm rings. Pass through the first seven beads strung in this step. Weave through the beads to exit from the common wall inside the following 9-mm ring of the circle. The second triangle is now complete.

11 Repeat steps 9 and 10 for a total of five triangles.

12 Weave through the beads to exit up through the common wall at the tip of one of the triangles. Pick up three size 15° seed beads and pass down through the same common wall to form a picot (figure i). Pick up three size 15° seed beads and pass up through the same common wall to form a picot on the other side of the common wall. Repeat the thread path of that entire triangle to reinforce the beadwork, switching to a size 13 needle if necessary to pass through the beads. Repeat this entire step to add two picots to each common wall at the center of the flower.

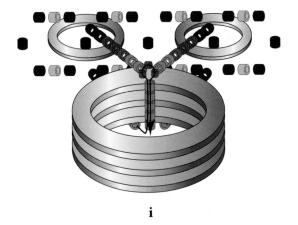

i

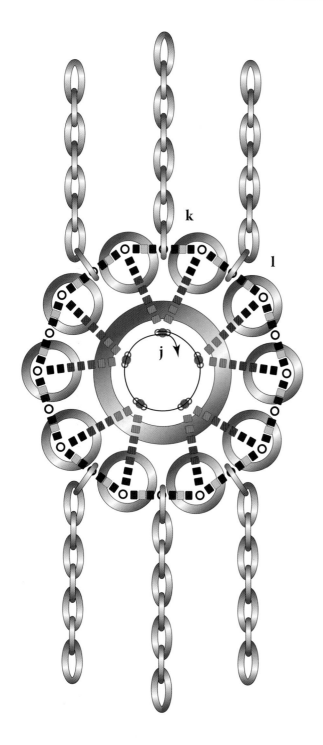

13 Exit from the top bead of the final picot. Pass through the top bead of each picot to form a circle (figure j).

14 Weave through all the units again until the beads are full of thread, giving the flower more body. Secure the thread and trim.

Assembly

15 Use one jump ring to connect a 2⅛-inch (5.4 cm) piece of chain to the beadwork between two 9-mm rings, inside one of the triangles (figure k). Cut two 2¼-inch (5.7 cm) pieces of chain. Use one jump ring to connect one end of a chain to the beadwork so that it sits between the next two 9-mm rings, flanked by two triangles (figure l); repeat on the other side of the 2⅛-inch (5.4 cm) chain already placed. Repeat this step on the opposite edge of the flower. Note: This bracelet is designed to fit snug so the flower stays on top of the wrist. Be sure to adjust the chain length to fit your wrist.

16 Use jump rings to connect the open chain ends on one side of the flower to the loops of one clasp half. Repeat for the other side, but add a dangle to each jump ring before closing. The weight of the dangles will help keep the flower on top of the wrist.

diamond ring

A diamond ring doesn't have to be
expensive. This chainmail version,
created with a base of peyote stitch,
can still be a girl's best friend.

diamond ring

Supplies

Dark blue size D nylon beading thread

Green-lined blue luster size 11° cylinder beads, 4 g

12 sterling silver 18-gauge open jump rings, 3 mm I.D.

Thread conditioner

Size 13 beading needle

Scissors

Thread burner

Clamps or bead stoppers

Various pliers

Techniques: Odd-count peyote stitch, square stitch, chainmail variation

Finished size: ⅜ inch (9 mm) wide

1   Place a clamp 6 inches (15.2 cm) from the end of 5 feet (1.5 m) of conditioned thread. Pick up eight beads. Pass back through the sixth bead just strung (figure a).

2   Pick up one bead, skip a bead, and pass through the next bead; repeat twice to work peyote stitch across the row (figure b). Remove the clamp.

3   Pass through the first, second, and third beads strung in step 1; the second bead added in step 2 (marked "10" in figure c); back through the second and first beads from step 1; and the last bead placed (marked "11" in figure c). This figure-eight turn-around positions the needle for the next row and is required for every other row.

4   Repeat step 2 (figure d).

5   Repeat steps 2 and 3 one more time.

a   b

c   d

6 Pick up one bead, skip a bead, and pass through the next bead. Make a "hole" in the beadwork by weaving through the next two beads. Pick up one bead, skip a bead, and pass through the next bead (figure e).

7 Pick up one bead, skip a bead, and pass through the next bead. Pick up one bead, pass back through the next bead in the row and through the bead just added to square stitch it in place (figure f).

8 Pick up two beads. Stretch the strand across the previous row and square stitch the second bead just added to the adjacent bead on the left. Pass through the next bead, and pick up one bead (figure g). Work a figure-eight turnaround.

9 Repeat steps 6, 7, and 8 (figure h). Repeat step 6 (figure i).

10 Work across the row in peyote stitch, ending with a figure-eight turnaround (figure j). Weave through beads to exit from the first bead added in the final row (figure k).

11 Pick up one bead, square stitch it to the adjacent bead to the left. Pick up two beads and square stitch the second bead just added to the next "up" bead in the last row; repeat across (figure l).

12 Repeat steps 10 and 11 in the opposite direction. Repeat, reversing direction in each row, until there are four rows with three holes each. Repeat steps 6, 7, and 8 to form two more holes (figure m).

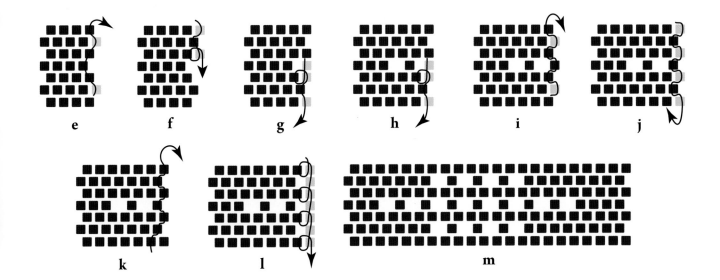

e   f   g   h   i   j

k   l   m

diamond ring

13 Work odd-count peyote stitch until the strip is long enough to wrap comfortably around your finger; end with an even-numbered row. Forty beads along the edge (a total of 80 rows) makes a size 9 ring; 41 beads along the edge (a total of 82 rows) makes a size 10 ring. Adding or subtracting two rows will change the ring about one size.

14 Fold the beadwork so the first and last rows meet, the beads interlocking like a zipper. Taking care that the strip isn't twisted, weave back and forth through the beads to close the beadwork into a tube (figure n). Secure the thread and trim.

15 Attach the 3-mm jump rings to the beadwork so they sit horizontally through the holes in the beadwork. The jump rings should form three parallel rows with two jump rings in the top row, four in the middle, and two on the bottom (figure o).

16 Use one 3-mm jump ring to connect each pair of jump rings placed in step 15 (figure p).

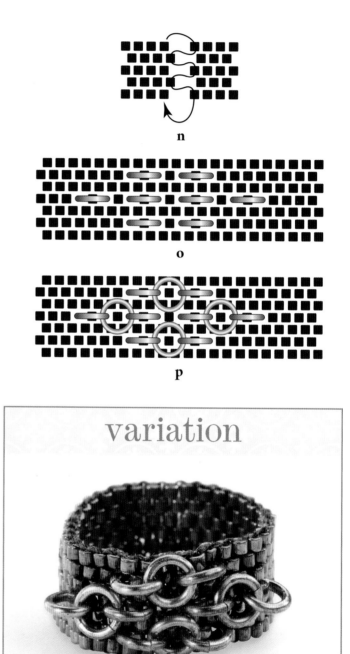

n

o

p

variation

musubu earrings

These earrings look complicated but are actually simple to make. They start with a base of beaded circles that is embellished with pairs of jump rings, creating a lovely knotted pattern.

musubu earrings

Supplies

Smoke 6-pound (2.7 kg) braided
  beading thread

Version 1

   Matte metallic blue/teal iris size 15°
      seed beads, 2 g

   60 sterling silver 18-gauge open
      jump rings, 3 mm I.D.

   2 sterling silver ear wires

Version 2

   Matte metallic purple iris size 15°
      seed beads, 2 g

   60 bronze 18-gauge open jump
      rings, 3 mm I.D.

   2 bronze or antiqued brass ear wires

Version 3

   Gold-lined peach alabaster size 15°
      seed beads, 2 g

   60 copper 18-gauge open jump
      rings, 3 mm I.D.

   2 copper ear wires

Thread conditioner

Size 12 beading needle

Scissors

Thread burner

Various pliers

Techniques: Right-angle weave,
   Japanese chainmail variation

Finished size: 1 inch (2.5 cm)

1 Thread the needle with 2 feet (61 cm) of conditioned beading thread. Pick up 18 beads, leaving a 4-inch (10.2-cm) tail. Pass through the first 11 beads strung to form a unit (figure a). The last two beads exited will be referred to as the "common wall" for this and subsequent units.

2 Pick up 16 beads; pass through the common wall and the first nine beads just strung (figure b).

3 Pick up 16 beads; pass through the common wall and the first 13 beads just strung (figure c).

4 Pick up 17 beads; pass through the bottom bead of the unit formed in step 3 and the first five beads just strung (figure d).

5 Pick up 12 beads; pass through the bottom bead of the unit formed in step 2. Pick up three beads; pass through the common wall and the first nine beads added in this step (figure e).

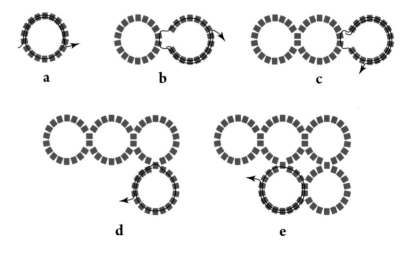

a　　　　　　**b**　　　　　　**c**

d　　　　　　**e**

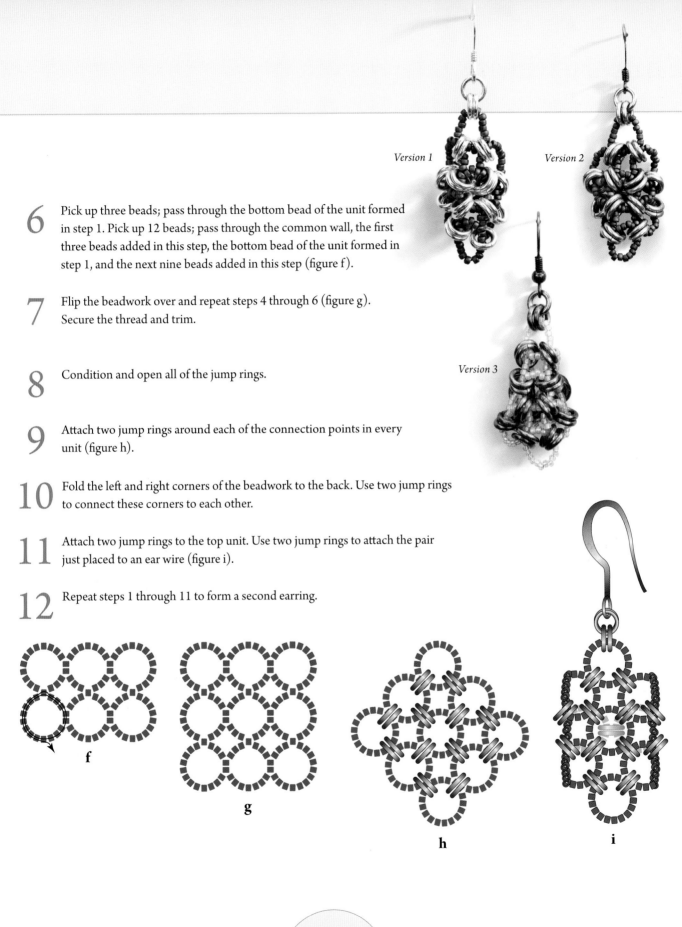

Version 1

Version 2

Version 3

6 Pick up three beads; pass through the bottom bead of the unit formed in step 1. Pick up 12 beads; pass through the common wall, the first three beads added in this step, the bottom bead of the unit formed in step 1, and the next nine beads added in this step (figure f).

7 Flip the beadwork over and repeat steps 4 through 6 (figure g). Secure the thread and trim.

8 Condition and open all of the jump rings.

9 Attach two jump rings around each of the connection points in every unit (figure h).

10 Fold the left and right corners of the beadwork to the back. Use two jump rings to connect these corners to each other.

11 Attach two jump rings to the top unit. Use two jump rings to attach the pair just placed to an ear wire (figure i).

12 Repeat steps 1 through 11 to form a second earring.

f

g

h

i

acknowledgments

Among the many people I'd like to thank, first and foremost is my husband, Mike, for letting me follow my dreams — even if it meant giving up a free company car. My wonderful kids, Keely and Connor, have been very understanding as I spent hours at the bead table or computer instead of doing fun stuff with them. To all of my parents — Mom & Chris, Dad & Patty — I thank you for your unconditional love and support. And to the rest of my family and friends, thanks for not getting too mad at me for not being around much for the last year.

To Stephanie, I am grateful you wanted to stop into a bead store that day to make a necklace for Baxter. Once I saw what you could do with those lovely little glass beads, I was drawn into a whole new wonderful world and I've never looked back. Karin, you helped me in infinite ways. I am especially grateful for the laughter and for my sanity.

To Paul & Linda and Nan & Bob: Thanks for your words of support that made me feel like I could do anything that I put my mind to.

I had amazing support with materials and tools for this book, including generous donations from Ray Grossman, inventor of the indispensable JumpRinger tool; TierraCast, creators of the lovely rings used in many projects; and The Ring Lord, who provided lots of jump rings.

At Lark Books, I am grateful to Marthe Le Van for her enthusiasm, to Terry Taylor for not pressuring me during this process, to Jean Campbell for cheerily reviewing all of the copy, and to Kathy Holmes for making the book look just right.

Thank you to my project testers: Carol, Sonja, Candace, Wendy, Matt, and Martha. You guys beaded like crazy and turned around quick comments on ridiculously short notice. A special thanks to Carol, who didn't really know how to bead before volunteering to help out but ended up making almost half of the projects in the book. You have always been there and have never given up on me. I love you! Even Mike broke out a needle to test the Triad Ring, and Keely worked from instructions (completely unassisted) for the first time — thanks, Sunshine!

I want to thank Wendy for believing in me and giving me great opportunities, without whom my whole beading career would not have ever begun, and to Scott for helping me to keep my business head on straight. To my co-workers, thanks for listening to me worry about my deadlines. Also, to all of my enthusiastic students at Brea Bead Works who kept asking me, 'When are you going to write a book?' Here it is! I hope you like it.

— Cindy Thomas Pankopf

about the author

Photo: Denice Woyski

Cindy Thomas Pankopf's 15-year career as a graphic designer is the foundation of her current profession as a jewelry designer and instructor. Cindy teaches classes incorporating her own beading designs in Brea, California, at the Bead & Button Show, and at Bead Away events. She is also a certified Senior Art Clay Silver Instructor and the founding President of the Art Clay Society of Orange County, California. Her designs have been published in *Bead & Button* magazine. To see more of her work, visit www.cindypankopf.com.

index

Awls, 12
Bails, 10
Bead caps, 10
Beading needles, 12
Beads, 8–9
    accent, 9
    cylinder, 9
    focal, 9
    spacer, 9
Beading thread, 10
    braiding, 10
    nylon, 10
Calipers, 14
Clasps, 10
Coil holders, 14
Crimp beads, 10
Crimping, 17–18
Cut lubricant, 13
Decorative rings, 10
Dowels, 14
Ear wires, 10
Files, 14
Findings, 10
Flex shafts, 14
Jeweler's saws, 13
Jump rings, 10, 20–21
    conditioning, 20
    making, 21
    opening and closing, 20
Loops, 18–19
Mandrels, 14
Materials, 8–11
Pliers, 13
Polishing pads, 14
Projects
    bracelets, 31–33, 39–47, 50–55, 88–91, 96–99,
        104–107, 112–116
    earrings, 46–49, 52, 56–57, 121–123
    necklaces, 22–30, 34–38, 58–68, 73–87, 92–95,
        108–111
    pendants, 100–103
    rings, 69–72, 117–120
Rotary tumblers, 14
Scissors, 12

Seed beads, 8–9
    Czech, 8
    Japanese, 9
Stitches
    peyote, 17
    right-angle weave, 16
    square, 17
Storage, 14
Techniques, 15–21
    bead weaving, 15
    crimping, 17–18
Thread burners, 12
Thread conditioner, 11, 15
Threading needles, 11
Tools, 12–14
Winders, 14
Wire cutters, 13
Wire protectors, 10
Wires, 10–11
    flexible beading, 10–11
    gauges, 11, 14
    metal, 11
Wirework, 18–19

It's all on www.larkbooks.com

Can't find the materials you
need to create a project?
**Search our database for craft suppliers
& sources for hard-to-find materials.**

Got an idea for a book?
**Read our book proposal
guidelines and contact us.**

Want to show off your work?
Browse current calls for entries.

Want to know what new and
exciting books we're working on?
Sign up for our free e-newsletter.

Feeling crafty?
**Find free, downloadable
project directions on the site.**

Interested in learning more about
the authors, designers & editors
who create Lark books?